The Politics of Europeanization and Post-Socialist Transformations

Other Palgrave Pivot titles

Madhvi Gupta and Pushkar: **Democracy, Civil Society, and Health in India**

George Pattison: **Paul Tillich's Philosophical Theology: A Fifty-Year Reappraisal**

Alistair Cole and Ian Stafford: **Devolution and Governance: Wales between Capacity and Constraint**

Kevin Dixon and Tom Gibbons: **The Impact of the 2012 Olympic and Paralympic Games: Diminishing Contrasts, Increasing Varieties**

Felicity Kelliher and Leana Reinl: **Green Innovation and Future Technology: Engaging Regional SMEs in the Green Economy**

Brian M. Mazanec and Bradley A. Thayer: **Deterring Cyber Warfare: Bolstering Strategic Stability in Cyberspace**

Amy Barnes, Garrett Wallace Brown and Sophie Harman: **Global Politics of Health Reform in Africa: Performance, Participation, and Policy**

Densil A. Williams: **Competing against Multinationals in Emerging Markets: Case Studies of SMEs in the Manufacturing Sector**

Nicos Trimikliniotis, Dimitris Parsanoglou and Vassilis S. Tsianos: **Mobile Commons, Migrant Digitalities and the Right to the City**

Claire Westall and Michael Gardiner: **The Public on the Public: The British Public as Trust, Reflexivity and Political Foreclosure**

Federico Caprotti: **Eco-Cities and the Transition to Low Carbon Economies**

Emil Souleimanov and Huseyn Aliyev: **The Individual Disengagement of Avengers, Nationalists, and Jihadists: Why Ex-Militants Choose to Abandon Violence in the North Caucasus**

Scott Austin: **Tao and Trinity: Notes on Self-Reference and the Unity of Opposites in Philosophy**

Shira Chess and Eric Newsom: **Folklore, Horror Stories, and the Slender Man: The Development of an Internet Mythology**

John Hudson, Nam Kyoung Jo and Antonia Keung: **Culture and the Politics of Welfare: Exploring Societal Values and Social Choices**

Paula Loscocco: **Phillis Wheatly's Miltonic Poetics**

Mark Axelrod: **Notions of the Feminine: Literary Essays from Dostoyevsky to Lacan**

John Coyne and Peter Bell: **The Role of Strategic Intelligence in Law Enforcement: Policing Transnational Organized Crime in Canada, the United Kingdom and Australia**

Niall Gildea, Helena Goodwyn, Megan Kitching and Helen Tyson (editors): **English Studies: The State of the Discipline, Past, Present and Future**

Yoel Guzansky: **The Arab Gulf States and Reform in the Middle East: Between Iran and the "Arab Spring"**

palgrave▶pivot

The Politics of Europeanization and Post-Socialist Transformations

Nicole Lindstrom
Department of Politics, University of York, UK

DOI: 10.1057/9781137352187.0001

© Nicole Lindstrom 2015

All rights reserved. No reproduction, copy or transmission of this publication may be made without written permission.

No portion of this publication may be reproduced, copied or transmitted save with written permission or in accordance with the provisions of the Copyright, Designs and Patents Act 1988, or under the terms of any licence permitting limited copying issued by the Copyright Licensing Agency, Saffron House, 6–10 Kirby Street, London EC1N 8TS.

Any person who does any unauthorized act in relation to this publication may be liable to criminal prosecution and civil claims for damages.

The author has asserted her right to be identified as the author of this work in accordance with the Copyright, Designs and Patents Act 1988.

First published 2015 by
PALGRAVE MACMILLAN

Palgrave Macmillan in the UK is an imprint of Macmillan Publishers Limited, registered in England, company number 785998, of Houndmills, Basingstoke, Hampshire RG21 6XS.

Palgrave Macmillan is the global academic imprint of the above companies and has companies and representatives throughout the world.

Palgrave® and Macmillan® are registered trademarks in the United States, the United Kingdom, Europe and other countries.

ISBN: 978–1–137–35219–4 EPUB
ISBN: 978–1–137–35218–7 PDF
ISBN: 978–1–137–35217–0 Hardback

A catalogue record for this book is available from the British Library.

A catalog record for this book is available from the Library of Congress.

www.palgrave.com/pivot

DOI: 10.1057/9781137352187

In memory of George and Shirley Janzen

Contents

1	Introduction	1
2	The Politics of Europeanization	5
3	The Politics of 'Europe' (1989–1996)	17
4	The Politics of Conditionality (1997–2004)	33
5	The Politics of Crisis (2007–2014)	53
6	Conclusions	74
	References	78
	Index	95

1 Introduction

Abstract: *The chapter sets out the book's main premise: that post-socialist transformations and Europeanization, instead of complimentary processes, can be politically incompatible, leading to different types of political conflicts over European integration. Comparing two most different welfare capitalist models, Estonia and Slovenia, the book argues that conflicts over European integration are shaped by collective ideas underlying a country's particular post-socialist transformation path and whether the EU is perceived to fall to the left or right of the national political economic status quo.*

Keywords: capitalist models; Central and Eastern Europe; Estonia; European Union; post-socialist transformation; Slovenia

Lindstrom, Nicole. *The Politics of Europeanization and Post-Socialist Transformations.* Basingstoke: Palgrave Macmillan, 2015. DOI: 10.1057/9781137352187.0002.

If one seeks to analyze the interplay between transnational and domestic factors, few better sites exist than the post-socialist states of Central and Eastern Europe (CEE). This is a region where far reaching domestic changes brought about by the demise of state socialism have gone hand-in-hand with rapid integration into a trans-nationalizing economy, the concurrence of which is unparalleled in other regions of the world. Here political economic paths have not only been shaped by domestic political conflicts and compromises, but have also been influenced by external actors, most significantly, but not limited to, the European Union (EU). If scholars of comparative post-socialist transformations were faulted for paying scant attention to external factors, scholars of EU conditionality have tended to err in the opposite direction. That is, studies of European influence in CEE often focus on the effectiveness of EU conditions at the expense of understanding the diverse political economic contexts in which EU influence plays out.

This book argues that post-socialist transformations and Europeanization, instead of complimentary processes, can be politically incompatible, leading to different types of political conflicts over European integration. These conflicts, I argue, are shaped by collective ideas underlying a country's particular post-socialist transformation path. With the demise of communist regimes, some CEE states followed a more radical neo-liberal transformation path involving rapid liberalization, deregulation, and privatization. Others fashioned a more gradualist strategy that used state power to simultaneously build market economies while protecting domestic industries and preserving social cohesion. Today, like in Western Europe, we can observe a variety of welfare capitalisms among CEE states (Bohle and Greskovits, 2012; Nölke and Vliegenthart, 2009). Scholars of Western Europe have demonstrated how welfare capitalist models shape member state positions towards Europe. For example, in more liberal market economies such as the United Kingdom, European integration has traditionally been portrayed in Thatcher's terms as 'socialism through the back door'. In more social market economies such as Sweden, on the other hand, further integration had been depicted as 'Anglo-Saxon capitalism through the back-door' (Hix and Goetz, 2000, pp. 4–5). In other words, positions on European integration depend in part on whether the EU is perceived to fall to the left or right of the national status quo. This book suggests that we can observe similar patterns of political conflict over European integration among post-socialist CEE states.

The book considers this argument through a comparison of two new EU (and euro) member states: Estonia and Slovenia. Each of the two small, newly independent states was heralded as an economic success story upon joining the EU. But each state can attribute its economic success to a very different transition strategy: Estonia pursued the most liberalizing reform agenda of all CEE states, and Slovenia one of the most gradualist and interventionist. With the start of formal EU accession negotiations in 1998, each candidate was pressured to adapt its emerging market economy differently. In general, the EU pushed Estonia to de-liberalize its economy, whereas in Slovenia it pressed for further liberalization (Bohle and Greskovits, 2012, p. 94). In each case EU conditions encountered significant domestic opposition. National 'architects of transition', technocrats and intellectuals who played instrumental roles in forging initial transformation paths, mobilized to defend their models against the alleged threat posed by Brussels. Moreover, given that political and economic transformations in each state occurred simultaneously with the process of nation-state building (in Slovenia's case for the first time in its national history), the identity of the nation-state became inextricably linked to the type of economic model pursued. That each country was heralded by outside observers as an economic 'success' contributed further to the impetus of elites and electorates alike to defend its economic model against any external threat.

The book develops this argument by tracing the process through which elites in Estonia and Slovenia ascribed different meanings to Europe and the EU over time. In the earliest stages of transition, I show in Chapter 3 how economic nations were construed more in opposition to federal socialist pasts (Soviet and Yugoslav respectively) than to any substantive, proactive ideas about Europe or the EU. Chapter 4 goes on to show how this changed once each state entered formal EU accession negotiations, when the EU moved from wielding 'passive' to 'active' leverage (Vachudova, 2005). Now 'architects of transition' began to portray particular EU pressures as threatening the core values underlying their respective post-socialist transformation paths. Chapter 6 considers the impact of the global financial crisis and subsequent fiscal crisis on Estonia and Slovenia. It shows that while the crisis hit each state hard, marking the most significant threat to their particular welfare capitalist models since gaining independence, the Slovenian model has undergone the most significant change. The book concludes by identifying the broader theoretical contributions of the book to our understanding of the role of ideas in our understanding of the politics of Europeanization and identifies areas for future research.

2
The Politics of Europeanization

Abstract: *The chapter sets out a framework for analyzing how 'Europe', and in particular the EU, is contested within and across an enlarged EU composed of diverse welfare capitalist models. Understanding European integration as an open-ended, contingent, political project, the chapter considers two dimensions of EU contestation: (a) left/right ideas on state intervention in the economy and (b) market-making versus market-shaping ideas on European integration. The chapter offers a constructivist political economy approach to EU political contention considering how domestic actors, namely post-socialist intellectual technocratic elites, ascribe the EU with different meanings depending on particular national, collective understandings about the ideal relationship between the state, market, and society.*

Keywords: domestic actors; economic nationalism; European integration; transnational capitalisms; varieties of capitalism

Lindstrom, Nicole. *The Politics of Europeanization and Post-Socialist Transformations*. Basingstoke: Palgrave Macmillan, 2015. DOI: 10.1057/9781137352187.0003.

This chapter sets out a framework for analyzing how 'Europe', and in particular the EU, is contested within and across an enlarged EU comprised of diverse welfare capitalist models. Underlying the framework is an understanding of European integration as an open-ended, contingent, *political* project. In particular, it builds on models of political contention in the European Union (EU) that focus on two sets of ideological factors: the appropriate level and degree of state intervention in the economy (the traditional left/right divide) combined with ideational struggles over whether European integration should be driven by market-making versus market-shaping principles. To understand ideational conflicts over the EU, we cannot limit our analysis to member states competing within a supranational sphere (the functional approach) or to party competition at the domestic level (the Europeanization approach). The chapter suggests that we need a more dynamic understanding of the politics of Europeanization that examines how domestic actors, namely intellectual technocratic elites, ascribe the EU with different meanings depending on particular national, collective understandings about the ideal relationship between the state, market, and society.

The politics of Europeanization

If national leaders long counted on a 'permissive consensus' among their citizens on matters related to European integration, since at least the passage of the Single European Act leaders face an increasing 'constraining dissensus' (Hooghe and Marks, 2008). From French, Dutch, and Irish voters voting down constitutional treaties in public referenda to the rise of Euroskeptic parties, European citizens appear less willing to give their leaders free rein in matters related to the EU (Ivaldi, 2006). Questions concerning the appropriate scope of EU competencies, its democratic legitimacy, and indeed its very existence are the subject of growing political debate (Wilde and Trenz, 2012). Political contention in the EU falls along two dimensions. What Mair (2007) terms the 'functional dimension' encompasses conflicts over the EU polity, including its underlying social purpose, degree of institutionalization, and future trajectory. The 'Europeanization dimension', on the other hand, involves conflicts over the infiltration of EU rules and norms into the domestic sphere.

EU scholars who study political contention tend to focus on one of these two dimensions: some examine conflicts within the European

Parliament and other supranational arenas (Hix, Noury, and Roland, 2007) and others examine patterns of political conflicts within domestic representative channels, focusing largely on political parties and public opinion (Szczerbiak and Taggart, 2008). Yet the two dimensions are interrelated. As Mair (2007, p. 9) suggests, without greater consolidation and extension of EU competencies, there would be little concern about EU penetration into domestic affairs. Likewise, domestic concerns about the penetration of EU rules and norms feed back into political contestation at the EU level. The politics of Europeanization can thus be viewed as a combination of these two dimensions. Understanding the supranational and national levels as interconnected does not treat the EU as an end in itself (as it is in typical European integration approaches) or as top-down constraint (as in Europeanization approaches). Instead it points us towards a more dynamic understanding of the politics of Europeanization, whereby the meaning of the EU is socially mediated within diverse national contexts (Hay and Rosamond, 2002).

In order to analyze patterns of political contention, we can start by mapping different positions on the EU, or sets of ideal typical ideas, beliefs, and principles about the underlying social purpose of European integration (Parsons, 2003; Jabko, 2006). The first relevant value dimension is along traditional left/right lines. In particular, we can differentiate among different ideas about how far the state should intervene in the market to promote collective goods (Hix, 1999, p. 73). A second dimension concerns ideas over the appropriate relationship between the sovereign state and supranational institutions. On one end of the continuum lies the belief that authority should reside in directly accountable national governments with few or no transfer of competencies to the European level, and on the other an allegiance to neo-functionalist ideas in which the gradual transfer of competencies to the EU should eventually lead to a single European polity and identity.

Hooghe and Marks (1999) offer a two-dimensional model of the EU political space whereby the left/right dimension and the sovereignty/integration dimension jointly structure actors' positions on the EU (Marks and Steenbergen, 2004, p. 10). They argue that as the EU seeks to expand its competencies over social market-shaping matters, left-leaning actors will become more pro-integration (what they term 'regulated capitalism') and right-leaning actors more anti-integration ('neo-liberalism'). Figure 2.1 adapts Hooghe and Marks' model to consider a wider range of positions. Left-leaning positions share in common a principled attachment to the idea that markets should be regulated in order to promote a range of collective goods. But they differ over the most appropriate site for exerting such authority. A 'national social model' advocates a strict decoupling between market integration at the European level and social protection at the national level (Scharpf, 2002). A 'European social model' position, on the other hand, is more skeptical of such a tidy decoupling. It suggests that as economic integration places increasing direct and indirect pressures on national welfare states, the only effective means of maintaining regulations and social protections is furthering social integration at the EU level.

Turning to the right-leaning end of the spectrum: right-leaning actors share an underlying belief in reducing or eliminating regulations and other restrictions on the free movement of goods and capital. But they differ over how truly free markets can most effectively be achieved. Advocates of a 'national market liberal model' argue that the best means of ensuring open markets is through global integration, ideally sidelining or, in some cases, exiting the EU. The UK Independence Party exemplifies such an approach. Those who support a 'neoliberal model', however, argue that furthering negative- or market-making integration at the EU, while obstructing social integration, presents the most suitable means of making member state governments more responsive to the discipline of transnational market forces.

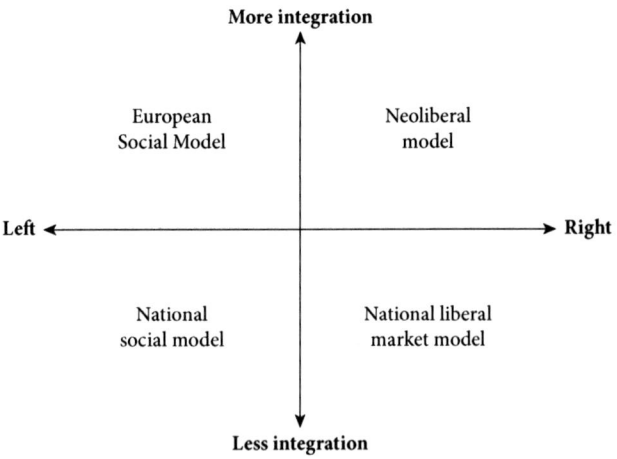

FIGURE 2.1   *Political economic positions on the EU*

Differentiating among these four ideal types makes two important contributions to mapping different types of political contention in the EU. First, many studies of Euroskepticism measure the intensity of anti-EU opinion, whether 'hard' or 'soft' (Szczerbiak and Taggart, 2008), 'specific' or 'diffuse' (Kopecky and Mudde, 2002). But such studies often fail to capture the *content* of this opposition. In other words, what type of 'Europe' in particular do actors oppose, whether specifically or diffusely? Second, in capturing variation in beliefs about the different goals of European integration (market-enhancing or market-shaping integration) and the means of achieving them (through European or national-level sites of authority), the model combines both the functional and Europeanization dimensions of political contestation. That is, ideological conflicts over the future trajectory of the EU are not limited to 'regulated capitalism' versus 'neoliberalism', as Hooghe and Marks (2008) and others suggest. Actors on the left and the right also disagree over which site of authority (national or EU) that political economic goals are best achieved.

To analyze these patterns of contestation, the book focuses on how different types of national welfare capitalisms shape positions on the EU. It builds on studies that focus on welfare capitalisms as an important intervening variable in mapping conflicts over European integration. Brinegar, Jolly and Kitschelt (2004: 86) show, for example, how different varieties of capitalism determine citizens' opinions on the EU. They find that in social democratic comprehensive welfare states such as Sweden, Denmark, and Finland left-leaning voters tend to oppose further EU integration. In liberal residual welfare states such as the United Kingdom, on the other hand, right-leaning voters are most opposed. In Christian democratic welfare states such as Germany, they find little right-left polarization on the EU issue. In another study, Ray (2004) finds that the more favorably voters view their current national policies, such as levels of spending on social welfare protections, the more likely they are to oppose ceding authority to the supranational level. A key conclusion of such studies is that critics of Europeanization are united by a desire to preserve the national status quo against any further intrusion of European rules and norms.

Focusing on types of national welfare capitalisms as a key determinant of European integration positions contributes to our understanding of political contestation in the EU in a number of ways. For one, it challenges conventional wisdom that the most strident critics of further integration are those on its losing end, such as lower skilled workers unable to compete in more open and integrated markets (Gabel, 1998). Instead it suggests that it may indeed be the 'winners' across European societies who are most reluctant to 'rock the boat' by transferring more authority to supranational institutions (Ray, 2004, p. 58). Second, while a majority of studies focus on political parties or public opinion, a political economy approach is well suited to analyzing the role of other domestic actors, such as political elites, public intellectuals, labor unions, business associations, and other civil society groups (Vasilopoulou, 2013). Menz (2003), for example, shows how trade unions in more liberal states are more inclined to advocate re-regulation at the EU level than their counterparts in more corporatist member states who fear a transfer of authority to the EU level would erode strong existing domestic regulations.

Finally such an approach acknowledges that while European integration has led to convergence in numerous policy areas, the EU remains comprised of diverse national welfare state models. As Scharpf (2002, p. 651) suggests, citizens are attached to, or 'embedded in' (Polanyi, 1944), particular historical understandings of the ideal relationship between the state, market, and society. These collective beliefs, in turn, carry a high degree of political salience, as citizens expect their states to protect them against the unfettered forces of market liberalization. Thus, opposition to European integration can be driven by concerns that the EU not only poses a threat to one's personal circumstances but also to the very social foundations of a particular national welfare state model.

The politics of Europeanization in CEE

A main contention of the literature on Europeanization of post-socialist states is that we can observe more limited domestic debate on European integration in new EU member states than in existing ones (Grabbe, 2003, pp. 305). Some scholars have attributed this outcome in part to the asymmetrical nature of EU accession process, whereby membership is presented as a take it or leave it proposition. That is, the EU sets conditions of membership and applicant states must comply in full in order to join the club, leaving little room for debating those rules (Mair and Zielonka, 2002, p. 2). Others suggest that even if space existed to contest Europeanization, domestic institutions are too unstable and civil society too weak to mount any significant protest or offer any alternatives (Grabbe, 2003, p. 306; Sissenich, 2007). Moreover, with CEE states relatively underdeveloped in socioeconomic terms, with lower wages, higher unemployment rates, and weaker social provisions than in Western Europe, defending the status quo appears less compelling (Krastev, 2013). Returning to Ray (2004), one might expect citizens in these states to *want* to rock the boat in the face of Europeanizing pressures.

If one focuses on formal compliance, then one can indeed observe a high degree of EU rule adoption across CEE states. Governments have met EU democratic conditions, parliaments have transposed thousands of pages of EU laws and directives into domestic legislation, and state bureaucracies have created new administrative institutions to implement EU rules and regulations. However, the overwhelming focus in the Europeanization of CEE literature on technocratic questions of legal or administrative compliance has often overshadowed questions related to the politics of Europeanization (Hille and Knill, 2006). Given that EU accession has exerted an impact on almost every domestic political institution and public policy, we would expect some degree of contestation over the terms and scope of the infiltration of EU rules and norms. We can thus pose the questions: to what extent have EU measures been contested domestically in CEE and on which dimensions? Does this map on to patterns identified in existing member states? To what extent can our multi-dimensional framework travel to post-socialist Europe?

Returning to the political positions on European integration outlined in Figure 1 above, I consider where political contention in CEE states is likely to be positioned along the two axes. Many observers of the region would predict that CEE states would gravitate towards the right-leaning, less-integration end of the spectrum. For one, decades of communist rule left most CEE citizens wary of state intervention of any sort (Marks, Hooghe, Nelson, and Edwards, 2006, pp. 160–161). Second, some suggest that states that regained independence from decades under the direct or indirect rule of Moscow (or Belgrade) would be more skeptical of transferring political competencies to another supranational entity, namely Brussels. Third, most post-socialist states were exposed to greater global influence in the early stages of transition in which the IMF and other actors promoted a 'shock therapy' programme of liberalization, privatization, and deregulation (Wedel, 2001). In sum, many observers argue that Eastern enlargement, by bringing in ten more neo-liberal oriented members, has further strengthened the position of those who resist expansion of EU competencies beyond the single market and weakened the European (and national) social model positions (Vaughan-Whitehead, 2003; Copeland, 2012).

While such accounts identify many important features of post-socialist transformations in general, they tend to obscure the varieties of capitalist models in CEE. As transition scholars have documented at considerable length, CEE states experienced communism and pursued economic and political reforms differently. While some states followed a neo-liberal development agenda, others fashioned a more gradualist strategy that used state power to simultaneously build market economies and preserve social cohesion (Bunce, 1999; Orenstein, 2001). Applying comparative capitalist frameworks to CEE, scholars argue that we can observe a similar diversity of models among new member states as we do in Western Europe. Bohle and Greskovits (2007; 2012), for example, categorize CEE states into three ideal types: the 'neoliberal' Baltic States, the 'embedded neoliberal' Visegrad states of Czech Republic, Hungary, Poland, and Slovakia, and 'neo-corporatist' Slovenia. Focusing more specifically on industrial relations, Feldmann (2007) applies a varieties of capitalism (VoC) approach to compare Estonia's liberal and Slovenia's coordinated market models (see Buchen, 2007; Adam, et al., 2009).

Given the diversity of capitalist welfare state models in CEE, we can analyze how they shape conflicts over European integration. But to understand new member states' positions on the EU, we must first take into account a number of particular features of post-socialist states. The first concerns sequencing of the formation of capitalist welfare states and European and global integration. West European welfare capitalist state emerged within a global 'embedded liberal' (Ruggie, 1982) international economic order whereby states were granted autonomy to pursue interventionist policies to protect societies against global liberalizing pressures. In Eastern Europe, on the other hand, national welfare capitalisms developed in tandem with their integration into a rapidly globalizing and regionalizing economy. The openness of East European welfare capitalist states to transnational forces have led some scholars of comparative post-socialist welfare capitalism to call for new categories that capture these different historical and structural factors. Bohle and Greskovits (2012) refer to varieties of 'transnational capitalisms'. Nölke and Vliegenthart (2009) coin the term 'dependent market economies' to distinguish post-socialist states from 'market liberal' or 'coordinated market' ideal types identified among West European states.

Although post-socialist welfare capitalisms cannot be understood without taking into account the influential role of transnational forces in shaping domestic institutions, it does not necessarily follow that post-socialist societies are less attached to or 'embedded' in particular national models. A second unique characteristic of post-socialist states is that the process of national welfare state development occurred simultaneously with the process of nation-state building. In the early stages of transition, some observers predicted that opening states to market forces would inevitably conflict with the process of building independent nation-states (Offe, 1991, p. 875). Yet the two processes are not necessarily at odds. Indeed, transition elites could portray free market reforms as crucial to both escaping the communist past and rejoining the prosperous West. They could also appeal to the organic unity of the nation as a means of diffusing opposition to destabilizing reforms (see Bohle and Greskovits, 2012). By tying economic policies to nation-state building, national elites can portray particular political-economic transformation paths as constitutive of national identities.

A final consideration concerns relevant domestic actors. As discussed above, most analyzes of political contention surrounding the EU focus on political parties or domestic actors such as trade unions and other civil society groups. In post-socialist states, however, political party systems remain relatively unconsolidated and labor unions and civil society weak. As Eyal, Szelenyi, and Townsley (1998) argue, in societies where no class of private owners existed before the introduction of market economies, technocratic intellectual elites emerged as the key actors in forging transition strategies and justifying them to voters. In most CEE states, struggles ensued over the pace and type of economic reforms, with 'shock therapy' advocates constrained by those promoting a more gradualist or social market orientation and vice versa. In other cases technocratic intellectual elites united around one common transition strategy, resulting in more policy coherence and continuity. This book argues that technocratic elites who played a central role shaping post-socialist transformations paths emerged as some of the most influential actors in domestic debates over European integration.

An economic nationalist approach

These unique features of post-socialist transformations make economic nationalism a particularly well-suited concept to analyze political contention around European integration. Scholars of economic nationalism examine how national economic models are linked to national identities, conceived in historical, political, cultural, and social terms (Crane, 1998). Such expressions of 'economic nationalism' are not necessarily opposed to liberal opening of national borders, as the concept's historical association with mercantilism suggests (Helleiner, 2002). Economic nationalism can be associated just as easily with market liberal economic models as it can with more interventionist or protectionist ones (Abdelal, 2001; Helleiner and Pickel, 2005). We can thus utilize an economic nationalist framework to analyze the different ways that national elites promote the protection of the 'nation' in the context of increased political and economic interdependence at the European level.

An economic nationalist approach shares three underlying assumptions. First, national economic identities, like all identities, are social constructions, conceived and propagated through a process of social representations and practices. The construction of economic nations is a general process, but each economic nation is constructed in particular, path-dependent ways (Crane, 1998). Second, economic nationalism is best defined by its 'nationalist ontology' rather than 'specific policy prescriptions' (Helleiner, 1994, p. 326). In other words, contrary to conventional understandings of economic nationalism as an alternative to liberal or Marxist paradigms (Gilpin, 1987), economic nationalism is a 'generic discursive structure', amenable to a variety of political economic ideologies or policy paradigms (Pickel, 2005, p. 8). Finally, economic nationalism is relational, in that an economic nation, like all nations, is defined in terms of identity/difference (Connolly, 2002). That is, an economic nation can be defined in opposition to an 'other' and, at the same time, in positive orientation towards another cultural space (Abdelal, 2005, p. 21).

To analyze how economic nationalism shapes positions on Europe, we must first examine the *content* of economic nations, or how political economic models are rooted in representations of particular national identities. Clift and Woll (2012, p. 313) suggest that studying the 'variations and evolution of economic nationalism requires a careful focus on national references...locating analysis historically and culturally within distinctive sets of state-society relations'. By focusing our analysis of economic nationalisms within state-society relations, we can demarcate the space in which nations are constructed and make comparisons across different national welfare state models. Bohle and Greskovits' (2012) Polanyi-inspired analysis of capitalist varieties is useful here. They categorize member states according to degrees and kinds of social embeddedness or how and to what extent states protect societies against the adverse effects of market integration. Polanyi himself never provided an explicit definition of society. Whether describing it as a 'relationship of persons' or 'social tissue' Polanyi's notion of society was defined more in opposition to the *homo economicus* assumptions of classical economists (see Lindstrom, 2011, p. 78). An economic nationalist approach focuses on how the 'social tissue' underlying welfare capitalist states is constituted in national terms (Abdelal, Blyth, and Parsons, 2010, p. 9). In particular, we can consider how different national identities influence the adoption and trajectory of different welfare capitalist paths (Blyth, 1997, p. 233). We can also, in turn, investigate how particular welfare capitalist varieties come to constitute an important aspect of national identity (Fougner, 2006, p. 179; Crane, 1998).

Economic nations are not static, coherent entities. A constructivist approach necessarily focuses our attention on the *dynamic* process through which these identities are constructed. One means of capturing this process is assessing how and to what extent the process of constructing the economic nation is 'integrative' or 'contentious' (Pickel, 2005, p. 13). Abdelal (2005, p. 25) suggests that in some cases ideas on what constitutes the economic nation are widely shared, and in other cases it is a source of considerable disagreement. Like many comparative political economy approaches, an economic nationalist approach assumes a certain degree of path dependency and cultural cohesiveness. In other words, underlying the vicissitudes of normal political competition lay deeper, more stable collective understandings about the norms and practices underlying national economies. Indeed, ascribing economic policies with a national social purpose can make change far more gradual, by lengthening time horizons for achieving social economic goals and legitimating economic sacrifices along the way (Abdelal, 2005, p. 26). But this does not imply that economic nations are 'immovable objects' (Pierson, 1998). As Tilly writes of nationalism in general:

> Like all culturally constrained social processes, nationalism proceeds in cultural ruts that greatly limit the directions it can go, relies on collective learning, but by its very exercise alters relations – including shared understandings – among parties to its claims. (Tilly, 1999, p. 418, quoted in Pickel, 2005, p. 8)

One concrete task is to identify 'parties to its claims' or bearers of nationalist ideas. In the case of post-socialist states, as discussed above, we can focus on technocratic intellectual elites as primary agents in constructing economic nations. The other task is to ascertain the extent to which these ideas encounter significant dissent, both from other elites and societal actors (Blyth, 1997, p. 246).

A final relevant feature of an economic nationalist approach is analyzing the relationship between internal and external factors in explaining *change* over time. Most institutionalist accounts of change in welfare capitalist trajectories have focused on domestic actors' responses to exogenous shocks, explaining change as coming from external pressures (Pierson, 1998; Schmidt, 2010, p. 5). Other scholars, however, offer a more endogenous account of change whereby external constraints are socially mediated. That is, domestic actors can ascribe similar external factors with different meanings, leading to different domestic outcomes (Cox, 2001; Blyth, 2002; Chwieroth, 2010; Berman, 2013, p. 232). Applying these insights to our analysis of the politics of Europeanization, instead of treating European integration as an inexorable external constraint we can investigate how common EU pressures are mediated by differently situated elites (Risse, 2001; Hay and Rosamond, 2002). The book argues that post-socialist states have been engaged in this battle of ideas since embarking on their quest in the late 1980s to return to Europe, and the following three chapters elucidate how.

3
The Politics of "Europe" (1989–1996)

Abstract: *This chapter examines how post-socialist leaders sought to establish their respective nation states as 'European' leading up to and immediately following the fall of the Berlin Wall. The chapter examines three discursive strategies deployed by CEE elites to secure their belonging in Europe: situating their nation at the center of Europe, the border of Europe, and in a sub-region of Europe. Through comparative case studies of Estonia and Slovenia, the chapter shows how these strategies served a dual function. Externally they were targeted to EU leaders to advance full and rapid inclusion into European institutions. Internally they were deployed to unify newly independent nation-states around a common European identity, often in opposition to 'other' outside (and in some cases within) national borders.*

Keywords: Clash of Civilizations; Cold War; Europeanization; return to Europe; Yugonostalgia

Lindstrom, Nicole. *The Politics of Europeanization and Post-Socialist Transformations*. Basingstoke: Palgrave Macmillan, 2015. DOI: 10.1057/9781137352187.0004.

This chapter examines how CEE leaders sought to establish their respective nation states as 'European' leading up to and immediately following the fall of the Berlin Wall. While most CEE elites embraced the discourse of the 'return to Europe', they did not necessarily specify to which kind of 'Europe' they sought to return. Meanwhile, European leaders were facing their own identity crisis as to what defines 'Europe' with the end of the Cold War. The chapter examines three discursive strategies deployed by CEE elites to secure their belonging in Europe: situating themselves at the center of Europe, the border of Europe, and in a sub-region of Europe. These strategies served a dual function. Externally they were targeted to EU leaders to advance their full and rapid inclusion into European institutions. Internally they deployed as a means of unifying newly independent nation-states around a common European identity, and most often in opposition to 'other' outside (and in some cases within) national borders. The next section outlines these three strategies more generally, before turning to an in-depth comparison of Estonia and Slovenia.

The 'return to Europe': three discursive strategies

The fall of the Berlin Wall in 1989 prompted euphoric declarations in Western and Eastern Europe that the continent, divided throughout the Cold War, would once again be 'whole and free'. Leaders of East European national independence movements rallied around slogans declaring their desire to 'return to Europe'. West European leaders responded in kind with promises to reunify East and West. French Prime Minister François Mitterand proclaimed in 1989, for example, that Europe would soon extend 'from the Atlantic to the Urals'. Once European leaders began to grapple with fashioning concrete policies for enlargement, however, contentious questions arose concerning boundaries (Where does Europe begin and end?), identity (Who is European?), and ideas (What is Europe?). When CEE leaders demanded a full 'return to Europe' most leaders were acutely aware that their national self-understandings as belonging to Europe did not necessarily correspond with external perceptions. As Gal (1991) suggests, the rhetorical slogan 'return to Europe' suggests such a duality, for one must return to a place where it currently does not belong.

The first discursive strategy involved re-positioning post-socialist states at the center of Europe. Beginning in the early 1980s, dissident intellectual elites from Czech Republic, Hungary, and Poland worked to revive the term 'Central Europe' to differentiate the Warsaw Pact states from the former Soviet Union (Schöpflin and Wood, 1989). In his essay 'The Tragedy of Eastern Europe', Kundera (1984, p. 33) explicitly defines Eastern Europe as Russia:

> As a concept of cultural history, Eastern Europe is Russia, with its quite specific history anchored in the Byzantine world. Bohemia, Poland, Hungary, just like Austria, have never been part of Eastern Europe. From the very beginning they have taken part in the great adventure of Western civilization, with its Gothic, its Renaissance, its Reformation – a movement that has its cradle precisely in this region. It was here, in Central Europe, that modern culture found its greatest impulse: psychoanalysis, structuralism, Bartók's music, Kafka's and Musil's new esthetics of the novel. The postwar annexation of Central Europe (or at least its major part) by Russian civilization caused Western culture to lose its vital center of gravity.

Kundera valorizes Central European cultural traits and intellectual accomplishments. In differentiating European from Byzantine culture, Kundera also continues an age-old exclusionary practice of forging European identity against a Russian 'other' (Neumann, 1999, pp. 65–112).

Establishing one's state at the center of Europe often involved arguing that it was *more* European, that is, civilized and advanced, than Europe itself. Kundera, by claiming that the 'cradle' of Western civilization lies in Bohemia, Poland, and Hungary, seeks to undermine popular associations of anything east of the Iron Curtain with unenlightened backwardness (Wolff, 1994). Many Polish elites, for example, believe that in the past Poland 'not only kept up with the West but even outpaced it in the development of liberal institutions' (Szacki, 1995, p. 45). These discourses can be read as a kind of national chauvinism. But they can also be interpreted as a kind of discursive strategy in which insisting on cultural parity or even superiority could help to balance out an inherently asymmetric relationship between the EU and aspiring members. We can also identify counter-narratives from those in the West seeking to challenge the glorification of Central Europe. François Bondy, for example, offers a riposte to Kundera's glorification of Central Europe as the heart of European civilization: 'If Kafka was a child of Central Europe, so too was Adolf Hitler' (quoted in Ash, 1990, p. 166).

A second and related strategy by which CEE elites promoted their entry into European institutions has been to situate themselves along the border of Europe. Connolly (1991, p. 64) suggests that the paradox of identity/difference is that 'identity requires difference in order to be, and it converts difference into otherness in order to secure its own certainty'. Applying this paradox to CEE states, post-socialist leaders attempted to secure their own European status by seeking to convert differences among post-socialist states to otherness. Moreover, by classifying neighboring states as 'non-European' CEE leaders could use borderland discourses to promote themselves as important defenders of Europe against the politically unstable and economically backward – in a word, less 'European' – regions to the east and south (see Razsa and Lindstrom, 2004; Lindstrom, 2003).

Todorova (1997) and others have shown how West European leaders have long sought to construct a positive image of Europe against others, whether Balkan or Eastern (see Wolff, 1994). CEE elites thus joined in a long European tradition by reproducing such discourses themselves. Bakić-Hayden (1995) describes a process of 'nesting orientalisms' through which national leaders in the Balkans construe their nation-state as more progressive, prosperous, hard-working, tolerant, and democratic (or European) in contrast to their more primitive, lazy, and intolerant (or Balkan) neighbors. Patterson (2003) shows similarly how Austrians and Italians often portray their Slovenian neighbors as Balkan, while Slovenians argue that the Balkans begin in Croatia, and so forth. While this endless chain of differentiation can occur between nations, it can also occur *within* nations. Residents in the more affluent sections of Ljubljana, for instance, suggest that the Balkans begin in poor housing estates with sizeable former-Yugoslav minority populations. In states with sizeable ethnic minorities the dominant ethnicity can be portrayed as more 'European' than the 'other within', such as Russian speakers in Latvia or Roma in Czech Republic.

This process of differentiation also has concrete political implications. For newly independent nation-states eager to join European institutions, portraying themselves as defenders of Europe's borders offered clear political dividends. Huntington's 'Clash of Civilizations' thesis was received so enthusiastically by many CEE elites because it reinforced their position within the borders of Europe (see Chirot, 1999). In response to the contentious question of 'Where does Europe end?', for instance, Huntington argues: 'Europe ends where Western Christianity ends and Islam and Orthodoxy begin' (Huntington, 1996, p. 35). Huntington's replacement of 'the rivalry of the superpowers' with the 'clash of civilizations' served as a useful means of refocusing the dividing line of Europe from ideology to culture (Lindstrom and Razsa, 1998). The Cold War logic of containment could also be sustained. As Huntington (1996, p. 34) remarks, Europe must now contain 'Islam's bloody border but also still significantly traditional cold war Byzantium enemies.' Many CEE elites eagerly embraced this role as the defense walls of Christian Europe, helping to make Huntington's thesis in a self-fulfilling prophecy.

A final discursive strategy used by leaders of aspiring EU members was to identify their states as belonging to transnational European sub-regions. This presented two main advantages. Like the previous two discursive strategies, it replaced the all-encompassing 'Eastern European' category with identities that had more positive connotations. Second, it was viewed as one means of improving the economic and political situation of one's state, either by banding together with similarly situated states and/or by creating closer links with existing EU members. With respect to Central Europe, Vaclav Havel (1990), argued, for example, that by transforming the region from a 'historical and spiritual' concept into a 'political phenomenon', CEE states could pool their economic resources and gain leverage as a political bloc. Only then, Havel suggests, could they approach Western Europe 'not as a poor dissident or a helpless, searching amnestied prisoner, but as someone who has something to offer' (quoted in Neumann, 1999, p. 155). Havel's vision moved a step closer to reality in February 1991 when heads of states of Czechoslovakia, Hungary, and Poland launched the Visegrád Group, a loose regional association named after the historic Hungarian castle-town. The Central European Initiative and the Central European Free Trade Area (CEFTA) followed in 1993.

Once the European Commission made clear that the EU accession process would proceed along a case-by-case basis, CEE leaders became more interested in developing strong bilateral relations with the Commission and individual EU member states than fostering cooperation among other applicants. If Havel had in mind Central European countries sailing towards the EU on the same ship, in practice EU accession looked more like a regatta of individual states desperate to get ahead of their competitors (see Böhmelt and Freyburg, 2014). Many CEE leaders found it more advantageous to associate with transnational sub-European regions, such as the Nordic Council or Alpe-Adria, which spanned the borders of East and West. Strengthening ties with existing EU member states through such regional associations promised more concrete rewards, such as support in EU accession negotiations and improved trade and investment ties.

The following section examines how Estonian and Slovenian elites drew on each of these discursive strategies in the early stages of transition. Like in CEE states more generally, Estonian and Slovenian elites identified their respective nation-states as belonging both historically and culturally to the center of Europe, each hoping to facilitate their rapid and full 'return' to European institutions. Returning to Europe in each case was inextricably linked with exiting socialist federations, the USSR and SFRY, respectively. Throughout the late 1980s and early 1990s, defining their particular nation-state as European was a means by which leaders could frame their quest for independence as a necessary emancipation from their Cold War past. The section examines how this process of differentiation focused not only on 'others' outside their national borders but also 'others within', namely Russians and 'Yugoslavs' who became minorities once each state seceded from their respective federations.

Estonia: from the Soviet Union to the European Union

Estonians quest to 'return' to Europe is inextricably linked to attempts to escape their Soviet past. Europe was framed as a 'savior' in such discourses, rescuing Estonia from decades under the rule of Moscow (Aalto, 2000). The inter-war period plays a central role in these discourses (Lagerspetz, 1999; Feldman, 2001). Admitted to the League of Nations in 1922, the Republic of Estonia enjoyed less than 20 years of sovereign statehood before the outbreak of the Second World War. After gaining independence in 1991, these inter-war years have been 'recast in a mythical light as an ultimate expression of Estonia's political and national identity'. Meanwhile Estonia's five decades under Soviet rule are portrayed as an 'unlawful occupation' (Viktorova, 2007, p. 46). Foreign Affairs Minister Toomas Hendrik Ilves describes Estonia's fate: 'In the wake of the Second World War, Estonia, Latvia and Lithuania were also the only European countries to simply disappear off the map when these three countries were forcibly occupied and annexed by the Soviet Union' (Ilves, 1998, p. 1). Estonia's return to Europe thus entails restoring Estonia to its rightful place on the map of 'European countries'. This section explores how Estonian elites used the three discursive strategies outlined above to accomplish this task.

With respect to positioning one's nation-state at the center of Europe, Estonian elites sought to establish Estonia as a fully European nation. Although it was more difficult for Estonians than Czechs to claim they belonged to Central Europe in strict geographical terms, Estonian elites nevertheless positioned Estonia at the heart of Europe. As Ilves (1998, p. 1) puts it: 'our identity is both geographically and spiritually a European one'. When Estonia submitted its application for EU membership in 1995, Estonian President Lennart Meri argued that Estonia has been part of Europe for many centuries:

> Estonia has belonged to Europe and been part of the Roman-Germanic legal system for over 700 years... This legal basis is a nursery from which everything else springs up. It is the prerequisite, the basis and very guarantor of the survival, the development, and success of our modern state. (quoted in Aalto, 2000, p. 3)

At other points Meri traces these origins back even further. On one occasion he remarks that 'it has been confirmed that the Estonians and Finns living on the coasts of the Baltic Sea can genetically be traced to the distant pre-history of Europe', and on another that Estonia has been integrated economically with Europe since the first century AD under the Roman Empire (Feldman, 2001, p. 10). Membership of present-day Tallinn (or 'Reval') in the Hanseatic League is also commonly evoked as evidence of Estonia's longstanding membership in Europe, with visitors to the Tallinn informed of the City Hall's Hanseatic origins.

'Europe' is not only invoked as an essential feature of Estonian identity; Estonia's return to Europe is also framed in opposition to the East. Huntington's 'Clash of Civilizations' found an enthusiastic audience in Estonia. At the launch of the Estonian translation of his book in 1999, Huntington travelled to Estonia to appear alongside Ilves and Prime Minister Mart Laar. Prominent political scientist and former leader of the Popular Front of Estonia (or *Rahvarinne*) in the 1980s and first Minister of Social Affairs, Marju Lauristin (1997, p. 34) writes in her edited volume *Return to the Western World*: 'Huntington's concept of civilizational conflicts as driving forces of historical development is supported by our experience'. She continues:

> From a cultural point of view, the Baltic countries, together with Finland and the Visegrad countries, represent the last resort of the Western-European Roman (Catholic and Protestant) cultural tradition located at the border of the Slavic Byzantine (Orthodox) world. (Lauristin, 1997, p. 35)

Lauristin's evocation of Estonia representing the 'last resort' of the West against the Orthodox word echoes a common refrain in Estonian discourse. Estonian speakers abroad often portray Estonia as a bulwark against Soviet or Russian spheres of influence. Meri, for example, uses this border metaphor when he remarks to a foreign audience: '[Estonia's] border is the border of European values' (quoted in Lagerspetz, 1999, p. 388). In a speech to the Swedish Institute for International Affairs, Ilves (1999) discusses Estonia's links with Finland and other Nordic states: 'Clearly the case is to be made that these Protestant, high-tech oriented countries form a Huntingtonian subcivilization, different from both its southern and eastern neighbors'. Ilves thus goes beyond Lauristin's distinction above – and indeed Huntington's notion of 'Western' civilization – to further differentiate Protestant Estonia from its Baltic neighbors where Catholics comprise from 25 percent (in the case of Latvia) to 80 percent of the population (in Lithuania).

This process of differentiation not only applied to an external other, but also served to justify Estonia's policy towards its 'other within', namely the Russian-speaking minority. Upon gaining independence in 1991 Russian-speakers comprised nearly 30 percent of the Estonian population. The multi-ethnic composition of Estonia was viewed as both a cultural and political problem. Culturally, Russian speakers are construed as non-Westerners who threaten to 'dilute the European character of Estonia' by subscribing to an allegedly more collectivist and authoritarian worldview (Feldman, 2001, p. 11). Politically, Russian speakers, with their 'undermined geopolitical orientations', were also portrayed as a security threat from within (Aalto, 2003, p. 583), an 'existential threat to the survival of the Estonian nation' (Viktorova, 2007, p. 46). An Estonian member of parliament who played a central role in writing Estonia's citizenship laws evoked Huntington, arguing that it is a 'ruthless fact' that a Russian considers 'a Serb a brother and an Estonian an alien', given that 'blood is thicker than water' (quoted in Feldman, 2001, p. 11). When the EU sought to work through the OSCE to reform Estonia's citizenship laws that disenfranchised Russian speakers who failed to pass difficult Estonian language tests, many Estonian critics now directed their ire at the EU as well as Russia. Instead of rescuing Estonia from the Soviet sphere, European leaders were accused of acting as an agent of Russian interests (see Kuus, 2002; Aalto, 2003).

With respect to the third discursive strategy, that is, identifying with transnational regional identities, two associations are most relevant in the case of Estonia: Baltic and Nordic cooperation. In terms of Baltic regional identity, Baltic cooperation has some historical precedence.

Before declaring independence in 1918, Estonian leader Jaan Tõnisson proposed creating a 'Balto-Scandian' federal state comprising 'the Estonian, Latvian and Lithuanian people along with Finland and Scandinavia.' In the 1930s Latvia, Estonia, Lithuania, and Finland a formed the Baltic Council, a security alliance designed to fend off Soviet and German advances. That Finland was considered a Baltic State before the war serves as a potent reminder for Estonians of their different fates over the next 40 years. As Ilves (1998) explains: 'I shall not dwell on the intervening horrors, except to say that in 1939, Estonia and Finland enjoyed the same level of development. Today, the difference between EU member Finland and Estonia are dramatic, to say the least'. Ilves sees Finland's 'successful self-redefinition as itself as a Nordic, not a Baltic country' as a reassuring example of how 'perceptions can change' (Ilves, 1998, p. 1).

By the mid-1980s, Estonian, Latvian, and Lithuanian intellectual and political elites sought to resuscitate the Baltic region as a distinct identity. Initiatives to re-create the region included series of conferences and seminars, articles, and community-building exercises such as a cruise around the Baltic Sea by nationals from all three states. One of the most visible examples of Baltic identity building was the so-called 'Baltic Way'. In August 1989, on the 50th anniversary of the Molotov-Ribbentrop Pact, nearly two million people joined a 600 kilometer human chain connecting Tallinn, Riga, and Vilnius. The protest bolstered the independence movements in each of the three states. The demonstration also projected an image of Baltic solidarity to foreign audiences (Taagepera, 1993, p. 156). Yet such efforts to create linkages among Estonia, Latvia, and Lithuania proved to have limited longevity after the fall of the Soviet Union. As one participant in one of these regional building conferences remarked, with a dose of sarcasm, 'hardly ever did such inter-Baltic enthusiasm exist earlier, either in the Baltic or in exile' (quoted in Neumann, 1999, p. 136). As Neumann (1999, p. 135) suggests, elites in these states were reluctant to 'put all their region-building eggs in one basket'. Belonging to the Nordic region offered many more advantages. Their Nordic counterparts, however, often exhibited a certain degree of ambivalence towards their newly independent Baltic neighbors (Wæver, 1992).

In some cases elites made up entirely new regions, such as Ilves invention of 'Yule-land'. He coins the term in relation to the historical practice of burning Yule-logs on the winter solstice, with 'Yule-landers' today using some variant of the word 'yule' to describe this practice. He explains:

> The Yule-swath that extends from Iceland and Britain through the Scandinavians to the Finnic lands that include Estonia, ends there... This cultural substrate would be interesting but meaningless, were it not very much in evidence today in the attributes others ascribe to Yule-landers and the quite measurable behaviour of individuals in the aggregate. Brits, Scandinavians, Finns, Estonians consider themselves rational, logical, unencumbered by emotional arguments; we are business-like, stubborn and hard-working.

Ilves' construction of Yule-land is significant for three reasons. The first is that Yule-land, unlike the Nordic region, encompasses the United Kingdom. Estonia's liberal economy makes it an anomaly among the more social democratic world of Nordic welfare states. By including fellow market liberal United Kingdom in Yule-land Ilves seeks to transcend such political economic differences. Second, Ilves' passage highlights the importance of both external and internal validation of ascribed regional characteristics. Not only are the attributes of Yule landers evident in the 'quite measurable behavior of individuals', according to Ilves; outside observers also 'ascribe' these values onto the region. Finally, in demarcating Yule-land as ending in Estonia, Ilves constructs this region against The Baltics. He elaborates:

> Unfortunately most if not all people outside Estonia talk about something called "The Baltics". This is an interesting concept, since what the three Baltic States have in common almost completely derives from shared unhappy experiences imposed upon us from outside: occupations, deportations, annexation, Sovietization, collecitivization, russification. What these countries do not share is a common identity... I think it is time to do away with poorly fitting, externally imposed categories. It is time that we recognize that we are dealing with three very different countries in the Baltic area, with completely different affinities. There is no Baltic identity with a common culture, language group, or religious tradition.

Ilves goes on to suggest that Lithuania, for example, is better suited to another region: Central Europe. 'Lithuania has been correctly pointing out that it is a Central European country', Ilves remarks. 'Its Catholicism, architecture, history all link it to Poland and the other Visegrad countries.' As for Estonia, Ilves suggests that Estonians are already described as 'the new Finns' (Ilves, 1999, p. 2).

Slovenia: from the Balkans to Europe (and back again)

Slovenia's secession from the SFRY and the process of establishing a newly independent nation-state was framed in terms of exiting from the Balkans and returning to Europe. Slovenian leaders evoked a range of historical and cultural criteria to insist that their decades-long membership in a Balkan federation was a historical anomaly. Slovenian President Milan Kučan remarked a day after Slovenia declared its independence: 'As a nation, which for more than one thousand years has been integrally involved in the development of Europe, we should like to be reintegrated into the best of the European tradition' (quoted in Rupel, 2000, p. 2). Like in other CEE cases, Slovenian elites argued Slovenia was positioned not at the periphery but at the center of Europe. As one editorial suggested, '... we should realize that we don't need to shove our way into Europe because we're already in it – and almost at its center, at that' (quoted in Vezovnik, 2010, p. 129).

In terms of historical criteria, many Slovenian commentators sought to establish a clear lineage where Slovenia's history was part of European history. One means of achieving this was linking Slovenian national identity to the medieval kingdom of Carantania, which included the present day territories of Austria, Hungary, and Slovenia. Carantania is construed as both the birthplace of the Slovenian nation and of modern democracy. One piece of governmental promotional literature from 1994 reads, for instance:

> The historical roots of Slovenian politics and democracy extend back to the 6th century, when the free kingdom of the ancient Slovenians – Carantania – was established. This kingdom was famous for its democratic institutions, strong legal system, popular elections of the ruling dukes and progressive legal rights for women. (quoted in Hansen, 1996, p. 475)

Slovenia, in other words, is not simply a passive importer of democratic traditions from Europe (let alone a Balkan authoritarian state). On the contrary, Europe inherited its egalitarian and democratic traditions from the Slovene kingdom of Carantania, including progressive legal rights for women. Bill Clinton, in the first visit of a United States' President to Slovenia, acknowledged this popular conception by expressing gratitude to his Slovene hosts for providing the democratic model on which

Thomas Jefferson based the United States Constitution (Lindstrom, 2003, p. 318).

Linking Slovenian national identity to Carantania serves two purposes. The first is to establish that Slovenia has historically always been part of Europe. The other is to imbue this European history with particular European values, namely a commitment to freedom, democracy, and human rights. Other commentators seek to tie Slovenia's European history to Slovenia's more recent past, namely 19th century nationalisms and WWII. One editorial in a leading journal remarks:

> From the days of Carantania, Trubar, the spring of nations in the mid-nineteenth century, the antifascist resistance in the mid-twentieth century, and the war of independence at the end of the twentieth century, it is clear that we are at home in the EU, although we never moved. (quoted in Vezovnik, 2010, p. 129)

What is notable about this passage is the inclusion of Slovenia's WWII history of anti-fascist resistance as evidence of Slovenia being 'at home' in the EU. While many Slovenians celebrate Slovenia's partisan history, linking Slovenia's partisan past to its European aspirations is by no means uncontested in Slovenian discourse. Many leaders on the right balk at attaching Slovenian identity to its Yugoslav past, appealing instead to religious or cultural criteria. As an editorial in the Catholic Church daily *Družina* (or 'Family') puts it: 'Even today the European soul is united. In addition to its common origins, it also has the same Christian and human values' (quoted in Vezovnik, 2010, p. 129).

Another discursive means by which some Slovenian transition leaders promoted their inclusion into European institutions was to identify Slovenian national identity as European in contrast to Yugoslavia and the Balkans. This discourse accompanied Slovenia's foreign policy towards the Balkans in the early 1990s that sought to disassociate Slovenia from the troubled region. Reflecting on Slovenian foreign policy successes in the decade following independence, Slovene Foreign Minister Dmitri Rupel writes:

> One particularly notable achievement of Slovene foreign policy is that, at the time of gaining independence, Slovenia as a state began to separate from the area to which it had belonged since the First World War, from the area which the Croatian writer Krleza lucidly called 'the Balkan pot-house,' in which Slovenia was a foreign body despite its proven adaptability over the years. (Rupel, 2000, p. 2)

Another editorial, written on the eve of Slovenia joining the EU seeks, to associate EU accession with a final extraction from the Balkans and Slovenia's Yugoslav history. He writes:

> Just a few more days and everything will be over: successful referendums will push us Slovenians into another world, where we will breathe freely among other (equal) European nations and where our Balkan adventures will be just a recollection of memories (of extortions, wars, murders, assassinations, etc.). This will be an exceptional historic leap. (quoted in Vezovnik, 2010, p. 130)

This association of Europe with equality and freedom as juxtaposed to the violent and unlawful Balkans is illustrative of the ways in which Slovenian leaders used the same kind of 'Balkanist' rhetoric Todorova (1997) identifies within Western discourse on the region. That is, the Balkans become a 'rhetorical repository of negative characteristics' against which a 'positive and self-congratulatory' image of one's European identity can be construed.

In terms of the final discursive strategy, sub-European region building, we can trace multiple processes within Slovenia, from Central Europe to Alpe-Adria and, notably, back to the Balkans. In the years leading up to and immediately following independence, many Slovenian elites embraced a Central European identity as an alternative to the Balkans, evoking historical and cultural criteria such as membership in Carantania to the Hapsburg Empire. A Slovenian National Assembly (1999) declaration put it bluntly: 'The Republic of Slovenia is a Central European country'. Slovenian leaders also emphasize their belonging to Mediterranean and Alpine regions of Europe, many of which preceded the dissolution of Yugoslavia. In 1978, for example, seven member states, including Slovenia, created the 'Working Community of Countries and Regions of the Eastern Alpine Area' [otherwise referred to as the Alps-Adriatic Working Community] to alleviate tensions between East and West, namely in regard to unresolved territorial disputes from the First and Second World Wars. Such regional organizations tend to be loosely organized and focus on cultural, environmental, tourism, and transportation-related issues. They also provided a useful means for Slovenian elites to re-position Slovenia symbolically as belonging to sub-European regions – the Alps and the Adriatic – located in the heart of Europe. Strengthening ties with Austria and Italy, especially when relations between Slovenia and the two states could be fraught over outstanding border issues, also promised to be helpful as Slovenia prepared its application for EU membership.

With respect to the Balkans as a sub-European regional construct: while many Slovenian leaders rejected such associations, this is not a universal stance in Slovenia. For many Slovenians their cultural and historical ties with the Balkans remain a positive aspect of Slovenian identity. Slovenian poet and essayist Aleš Debeljak in his *Twighlight of the Idols* offers, for example, a melancholic and nostalgic parting tribute to Yugoslavia. Debeljak laments the loss of the multicultural diversity of SFRY:

> For me, popular slogans about the 'celebration of diversity' were never mere philosophical speculation. As far back as I recall, these differences were the crux of my experience of life at a crossroads of various cultures... Yugoslavia was like a many-colored carpet that allowed me to maintain contact with lands that were dramatically different from the baroque Central European town where I grew up yet was still part of the same country. (Debeljak, 1994, p. 23)

Notably here Debeljak celebrates the cultural diversity of Yugoslavia but at the same time insisting that these lands were 'dramatically different' from his own 'baroque Central European town' of Ljubljana. Such expressions of 'Yugonostalgia' are a salient feature of Slovenian discourse, presented as an alternative to both exclusive nationalist discourses and to the wholesale denigration of Slovenia's Yugoslav past. A member of a Slovenian Yugonostalgic rock band expresses nostalgia for the SFRY that goes beyond memories of Yugoslav culture and everyday life:

> We all had a certain pride. We were raised to believe that Yugoslavia was a powerful country, a big country, and a beautiful country. That was a great feeling... now there is none of that. Slovenia is now an unimportant, peripheral and parochial country, often confused with Slovakia, (Lindstrom, 2006, p. 236)

These forms of cultural engagement with the Balkans were followed by formal political and economic ties. After the 1995 Dayton Agreement brought some stability to the region, Slovenian firms sought to increase exports to the important former-Yugoslav market (Svetličič and Rojec, 2003). With the exception of the short-lived right-wing Bajuk government in 1999, which froze Slovenia's participation in all Balkan regional associations, Slovenian governing elites pledged their support for Slovenia's active engagement in the region. The Slovenian National Assembly (1999), for example, declared that 'Through its active role and support to democratic processes in this area, Slovenia is establishing itself as an important and reliable partner of the international community in settling this situation in this part of Europe'. What is notable here is that Slovenian leaders argue that they are a vital and trustworthy partner of the *'international community'*, thus positioning Slovenia outside the Balkans and within European and international spheres.

While Slovenian leaders began to promote Slovenia as a 'bridge' or a 'translator' between Europe and the Balkans, the fear of being associated as a Balkan state remained. For example, Slovenia was the only state in the region not to send head of state to the Balkan Summit in Zagreb in 2000. Slovenian journalist Igor Mekina (2000) argued it was a premeditated move on the part of the government to ensure that Slovenia would not be recognized by the West as a Balkan state. Mekina also notes with irony that given Slovenian leaders posturing as 'European', most of their fellow European leaders were in attendance. Mekina goes on to suggest that the short-term benefits to ruling elites of gaining favor with the 'xenophobic strata' of the Slovenian public comes at the expense of Slovenia's long-term trade interests in the Balkans. Still by 2000 a prominent headline in the mainstream Slovenian weekly *Delo* in 2000 read, for example: 'Time to Europeanize the Balkan Café'. The article was accompanied by an editorial decrying the large number of Bosnian grilled fast food stands one can find throughout Ljubljana and the relative dearth of Viennese-style coffee houses (see Lindstrom, 2003).

Concluding remarks

We can draw three main insights from this chapter. First, discursive strategies related to the 'return to Europe' highlight a tension between an insistence that one's nation-state is fundamentally European and, on the other hand, awareness that one's European status is never ontologically secure (Razsa and Lindstrom, 2004). CEE leaders strive to make Europe something historically and geographically concrete, yet recognize that some countries are considered more 'European' than others in the perceptions of West European leaders. Efforts by Estonian and Slovenian leaders to distance themselves from the Baltics or the Balkans are motivated in part by concerns that they may end up on the 'wrong' side of the constantly shifting borders of Europe.

Second, Kuus (2002) identifies a puzzle in 'return to Europe' narratives in CEE: nation-state identities are construed in ethnically exclusively terms while, at the same time, framed in terms of belonging to a supranational and multi-ethnic construct (i.e., 'Europe'). This paradox can be understood if we consider how all identities, including 'European', are constructed in relation to an 'other'. If Estonian leaders define Estonian identity in opposition to Russia, this is consistent with the central role that Russia has played in European identity formation over centuries (see Neumann, 1999, pp. 65–112). Similarly, the way in which Slovenian leaders construct Slovenia identity in opposition to the Balkans resonates with the way in which the Balkans have been construed as Europe's 'other within' (Todorova, 1997). In this way, defining one's nation as European in culturally exclusive terms can be considered quite consistent with the 'Europeanization' of national identities.

Finally, all CEE leaders declare a desire to 'return to Europe'. Yet they ascribe 'Europe' with different meanings. Some focus on a cultural essence of European 'civilization' defined in broad historical or religious terms. Such discourses are consistent with Huntington and others who seek to define Europe by its Christian heritage and justify excluding applicants such as Turkey on religious grounds. Other CEE leaders imbue 'Europe' with liberal values such as a respect of the parliamentary rule of law, democratic norms, and social and human rights. In some cases, such as some Slovenian elites embracing Slovenia's Yugoslav Partisan past, Europe is defined in terms its struggle against fascism. The polyvalent character of European identity allowed CEE elites across the political spectrum to imbue national identities with very different values yet all under the discursive umbrella of 'Europe' (Razsa and Lindstrom, 2004). Yet once these states embarked on the more concrete tasks involved in EU accession negotiations, these different conceptions of 'Europe' started to focus more on the political-economic content of European integration. The next chapter explores this next stage of the Europeanization process.

4
The Politics of Conditionality (1997–2004)

Abstract: *This chapter examines the emergence of new patterns of contention around the EU as post-socialist states entered formal EU accession negotiations and the attention shifted from a 'return to Europe' to 'joining the EU'. Challenging accounts of the EU accession process as a largely technocratic process, this chapter argues for a more political and social understanding of this process. Tracing political debates over EU conditions in core EU policy areas (trade and competition policy), the chapter shows how 'architects of transition' in Estonia and Slovenia contested EU conditions when they were deemed to conflict with particular national welfare capitalist paths.*

Keywords: Banking privatization; Estonia; EU conditionality; Europeanization; Slovenia; varieties of capitalism

Lindstrom, Nicole. *The Politics of Europeanization and Post-Socialist Transformations.* Basingstoke: Palgrave Macmillan, 2015. DOI: 10.1057/9781137352187.0005.

The last chapter showed how in the earliest stages of transition, 'Europe' served as a broad category of meaning that CEE elites could use to legitimate their particular post-socialist transformation path. The EU for its part exerted only 'passive leverage' (Vachudova, 2005) or served as an 'inspiration' (Jacoby, 2006) for democratic and free market reforms but did not intervene directly to shape them. This changed once the states entered formal EU accession negotiations where attention shifted from a 'return to Europe' to 'joining the EU'. Now the EU could exert more active leverage over CEE states as post-socialist leaders worked to meet all the conditions of membership. Many observers have portrayed the EU accession process as a largely technocratic one: actors share basic policy goals (joining the EU), neatly compartmentalized into different issues areas (chapters of the *acquis communitaire*), and achieved through largely rational, technocratic means where decision makers are largely insulated from popular pressures (Schimmelfennig and Sedelmeier, 2005). This chapter argues for a more social and political understanding of this process, showing how Estonian and Slovenian elites contested conditions related to core EU policy areas (trade and investment) when they were deemed to conflict with particular national welfare capitalist paths.

Europeanization by EU conditionality

Europeanization frameworks were first derived and applied within the context of West European states (see Cowles, Caporaso, and Risse-Kappen, 2001). By the end of the 1990s many scholars turned their attention to analyzing the influence of the EU on candidate countries of Central and Eastern Europe (see Schimmelfennig and Sedelmeier, 2005). Although not full EU members, the EU accession process demands far-reaching changes in almost every aspect of the applicant's state's domestic institutions and rules. Since then numerous edited volumes, monographs, comparative analyses, and single-case studies assess the impact of the EU on a range of topic areas, from democratization and minority rights to banking regulation and environmental policy (for an overview of this now extensive literature, see Sedelmeier, 2009; Börzel, 2011). Similar to the Europeanization literature applied to West European states, the central question guiding such studies is what factors can account for variation in EU influence across time, countries, and policy areas.

When applying Europeanization frameworks to post-socialist states, scholars argue that we must take into account a number of significant differences between member and applicant states. For one, as non-EU members, applicant states play no part in shaping the EU rules and norms to which they are required to adhere. EU membership is presented as a 'take it or leave it' proposition: the EU sets the conditions of membership and applicant states must comply in full (Mair and Zielonka, 2002, p. 2). The process of change is thus more unidirectional in the case of candidate countries. While existing EU members can 'upload' preferences to the EU, candidate states are limited to 'downloading' existing decisions (Radaelli, 2003). A second difference is the means through which the EU enforces compliance with its rules. In member states, the EU relies primarily on domestic interest groups to monitor compliance. In applicant states, however, the European Commission assumes a more direct and invasive role (Sedelmeier, 2009, p. 5). The Commission can also use membership conditionality to induce change in areas, like democratization or minority rights, where it has no formal authority (see Kelley, 2004). Finally, scholars suggest decades of state socialism left East European economies underdeveloped, political institutions in flux, and civil society far weaker than in their West European counterparts. Some argue that the lack of well-established domestic veto points gives applicant state governments more freedom to implement EU decisions since they face less domestic resistance than do West European EU members (Grabbe, 2003, p. 306).

Given these alleged differences between EU member states and applicant states, some scholars argue that conditionality frameworks are more relevant than Europeanization frameworks in understanding the EU's impact on aspiring members. A central question guiding the EU conditionality literature is under which conditions EU influence is most effective in bringing about domestic change. The so-called 'external incentives model' has emerged as one of the most influential analytical approaches (Schimmelfennig and Sedelmeier, 2004; see Böhmelt and Freyburg, 2014, p. 2). The dependent variable in such analyzes is typically compliance or non-compliance with a particular EU condition at a particular point in time. Some scholars have distinguished further between formal change, or the legal transposition of rules, and more substantive change, namely the capacity to implement and enforce the rules (Schimmelfennig and Sedelmeier, 2004, p. 664). Others consider more far-reaching change. Vachudova (2005), for instance, considers the extent to which EU conditionality led to a convergence towards liberal democracy in EU candidate countries.

To explain variation in EU influence across candidate states, the external incentives model focuses first on EU-level variables. Conditionality is argued to be more effective when candidates understand what changes they must make to be eligible for membership and the time frame in which they must carry them out. EU rewards for compliance must also be both credible and timely. According to this argument, conditionality is unlikely to achieve its aims without a sincere promise of full EU membership. Schimmelfennig, Engert, and Knobel (2003) find, for example, that EU democratic conditionality was more successful in bringing about change in states like Slovakia and Latvia that received credible offers of membership than in Turkey whose membership the EU has continually delayed. Vachudova (2005) argues the type of EU leverage matters, with 'active leverage' exerted during formal EU accession negotiations proving more effective than 'passive leverage' in ensuring governments live up to core liberal democratic values.

Conditionality frameworks also examine a range of domestic variables to explain variation in compliance. According to the external incentives model, EU conditionality is likely to be more effective the lower the potential political costs of compliance for the respective government (Schimmelfennig, Engert, Knobel, 2003, p. 496). Given the strong pull of EU membership, domestic veto players rarely completely derail a state's quest to join the EU. Nor do most elected officials fear that complying with a particular EU condition, however politically controversial, would cost them their seats. But the presence of strong domestic veto players can arguably delay compliance with particular pieces of legislation or prolong controversial political changes required by the EU. Strong domestic veto players can also contribute to outcomes where the government formally complies with EU rules and conditions, but subsequently finds it difficult to implement and enforce them (see Falkner and Treib, 2008).

Potential domestic adoption costs vary across issue areas. Domestic adoption costs are likely to be higher the more politically salient the issue, or the degree to which a policy attracts the interest of powerful domestic actors or the public. Technical EU policy areas such as fisheries or anti-trust legislation, for example, will likely attract the attention of a small group of domestic experts, but pose few 'costs' to the government in terms of sparking public opposition. EU-inspired changes in labor or social policy, on the other hand, is likely to mobilize a wider range of actors, including various employer and labor associations, as well as the general public. Jacoby's (2004) notion of 'actor density', or the number of state and societal actors involved in a particular policy area, captures such a variable. Considering the degree of domestic salience of an issue helps us to ascertain the likelihood that actors will mobilize to contest the adoption of particular EU rules or seek to reshape the scope or type of change (Jacoby, 2004, p. 10).

The main conclusion of this literature is that EU conditionality has served as a very effective tool in influencing domestic change across post-socialist states, but under certain conditions, namely where the EU makes a credible commitment to full membership and where the domestic costs of compliance are not prohibitively high (Sedelmeier, 2009, p. 19). EU conditionality has also been celebrated by academics and practitioners alike for its general effectiveness as a foreign policy tool, highlighting the remarkable degree of domestic change across post-socialist states, whether consolidating democracy, protecting minorities, or creating competitive and well-functioning market economies. As to the question of whether such changes have endured after EU accession, scholars of conditionality offer a sanguine assessment: new member states generally register higher levels of compliance with EU legislation than longstanding EU members (Sedelmeier, 2012).

The Politics of conditionality

The conditionality literature shares with Europeanization accounts a move in EU studies towards what Gourevitch (1978) terms the 'second image reversed': an examination of the international sources of domestic politics. A Europeanization approach in general offers a number of advantages. First, by holding the 'EU' as a constant, Europeanization frameworks provide a useful analytical framework to compare the influence of the EU across member states, time, and/or policy areas, including those falling under new modes of governance such as the Open Method of Coordination. Second, while the EU compliance literature has long mapped different rates of compliance across EU member states, Europeanization frameworks offer more robust explanatory frameworks to assess why states comply or fail to comply. They draw our attention to important intervening variables, such as domestic veto players and coordinating institutions. Third, the extension of Europeanization frameworks to non-member states, with modifications as outlined above, demonstrates the ability of the framework to 'travel' without a significant amount of conceptual stretching.

The Europeanization framework has been subject to many criticisms, however, many of which can be extended to the conditionality literature. Some argue that by treating the EU as an independent variable, Europeanization approaches neglect to consider how EU demands are not necessarily fixed (Wincott, 2003, p. 279). The concept of 'goodness of fit' is illustrative. The hypothesis posits that the better the fit between a particular EU policy and the domestic status quo, the less likely a member state will encounter difficulties complying, whereas the worse the fit, the greater the need for a transformation in national policies and practices. But some argue that the 'goodness of fit' is not a simple matter of objective assessment; both EU policy and the 'domestic status quo' are open to interpretation and political debate (Mastenbroek and Kaeding, 2006). This leads to a second related criticism. An implicit assumption of much of compliance literature is how 'misfits' can be overcome to bring about EU-inspired domestic change. In a review of the Europeanization literature, Mair (2004, p. 347) argues that this 'rational, technocratic, chain-of-command logic' tends to reflect broader moves towards the depoliticization of decision making: both by accepting the EU as a 'polity without politics' and by reducing domestic politics to matters of 'administrative efficiency or institutional appropriateness'. In other words, it seems to leave little room for analyzing the politics of Europeanization.

To what extent can this criticism of the Europeanization literature more broadly be applied to the conditionality literature in particular? A strictly 'top-down' Europeanization framework where the 'EU' is held constant appears even more applicable to CEE states. EU conditions are clearly set out in the Copenhagen Criteria and the *acqui communitaire*, and the European Commission not only monitors but can also enforce compliance. The Commission's annual accession reports enumerate areas where applicant states have met the conditions and highlight problems that require change. In terms of explanatory factors for degrees of change, adoption costs or the 'enforcement' approach has dominated the conditionality literature. But other scholars point to administrative efficiency as being the main impediment to change among applicant states, summed up by Hille and Knill's (2006) declaration, 'It's the bureaucracy, stupid'. An underlying assumption of both the enforcement and management approaches is that applicant states view EU membership and EU rules positively; the problem lies in overcoming domestic resistance or developing the administrative capacity to implement them properly (Böhmelt and Freyburg, 2014, pp. 14–15; Falkner and Treib, 2008).

An explanatory factor largely missing from the conditionality literature is legitimacy, or whether domestic actors in CEE, like their West European counterparts, can exhibit 'obstinacy' when they deem EU rules and norms as illegitimate (Börzel et al., 2010). An important exception is Epstein's (2006) focus on 'normative consistency' as a factor in explaining domestic change across CEE applicant states. Epstein argues that EU conditionality must have legitimacy in order to produce an intended effect. An EU condition is more likely to be viewed as legitimate by domestic actors when EU members already fully adhere to what the EU is demanding of candidates. It also depends on the extent to which consensus exists within the EU on the technical or political correctness of a particular policy (Epstein, 2006, p. 5; Bruszt, 2002; Sasse, 2008). Thus the lower the degree of normative consistency around an EU policy, as in the case of agriculture, the higher is the chance that actors within candidate countries will seek to resist EU pressures. Where there is a high degree of normative consistency in a policy area, such as central bank independence, on the other hand, domestic actors face a more limited scope to oppose such measures or to make legitimate claims on the government to delay conforming to EU rules. Epstein's focus on the normative consistency of EU demands not only accounts for important variations among types of EU policies and how they may influence types of domestic change but it also considers how EU rules are contested, a dimension often lacking in more technocratic accounts of EU conditionality and compliance.

More ideational or constructivist accounts of EU conditionality literature help us to uncover ways in which actors in EU accession states challenge the legitimacy of EU rules. This shifts the focus of our study of conditionality away from strict compliance, or whether EU legislative rules were transposed into domestic law and implemented. Instead it focuses on ways in which actors resisted rules throughout the EU accession process, thus elucidating the 'substantive positions' (Mastenbroek and Kaeding, 2006) or strong preferences and beliefs of CEE actors. One advantage of such an approach is that while non-EU members cannot 'upload' preferences to the EU, it provides a basis for understanding how these new EU member states are likely to engage in ongoing EU debates as full members. A second advantage is more normative. As Raik (2004) argues, when the EU accession process was driven by the principles of 'inevitability, speed, efficiency and expertise', it constrained democratic deliberation over a wide range of issues central to the functioning of CEE political economies and societies. The academic literature on conditionality has tended to reproduce rather than rectify this democratic deficit. Analyzing how EU rules and norms were contested, even if the outcome was legislative compliance, can enrich our understanding of the political process of EU accession.

The following two case studies compare how EU pressures related to economic chapters of the *acquis* (including trade and competition policy) were contested within Estonia and Slovenia. In each case the Commission identified some degree of 'misfit' between the EU condition and the domestic status quo. Yet in each case domestic actors offered substantive positions on both the EU condition and how it threatened to affect the domestic status quo. The focus on single-market policies provides a number of advantages. For one, 'negative integration', or the removal of barriers to free movement of capital and goods, is central to the functioning of the EU. Surprisingly few studies on EU conditionality in CEE focus on these issues, however, a gap this book seeks to address (Sedelmeier, 2009, pp. 14–15). Moreover, analyzing how elite actors confront the core functions of the EU provides the most accurate means of assessing both left/right and more-integration/less-integration positions.

Contesting the EU from the right: the case of Estonia

Estonia's 'return to Europe' cannot be disentangled from its exit from the Union of Soviet Socialist Republics (USSR). As discussed in Chapter 2, Europe was framed as a savior in the early stages of transition, as a means for Estonia to escape its geopolitical position in the post-Soviet sphere. Although Estonia was the most economically developed Soviet republic, it was fully integrated into a rigid system of central planning, leaving it unprepared to compete in open markets. When Estonia seceded in 1991, exports outside the Soviet Union accounted for only two percent of the Estonian GDP (Feldmann and Sally, 2002, p. 90). The Russian economic blockade of the three Baltic States in 1991 had catastrophic effects: between 1990 and 1994, industrial production declined by 60 percent, gas prices jumped by more than 10,000 percent, and inflation ran at more than 1,000 percent per year (Lieven, 1993, p. 10).

Estonia's economic strategy at this critical juncture was based on a radical withdrawal of the state from the economy and a rapid opening of its markets (Smith, 2002). Key characteristics of this 'shock therapy' approach were the full liberalization of prices and trade. State trading monopolies and import quotas inherited from the USSR period were quickly abolished. None of these quotas were converted into tariffs. On the contrary, by 1993, Estonia had abolished *all* tariff and non-tariff barriers to trade, including on agricultural products. In addition, Estonians pursued rapid privatization and quickly passed laws treating foreign and domestic investors equally. As a result, foreign owners played a prominent role in the Estonian privatization process, purchasing around 40 percent of the sale value of all privatized enterprises by the end of 1994 (Haavisto, 1997). Consistent with this approach, poorly performing firms that failed to attract foreign investors were not extended government subsidies and allowed to fail.

One key factor in Estonia embarking on this radical neo-liberal path lies in its relationship to its Soviet past. The Estonian movement for independence in the 1980s was framed as achieving liberation from 'Soviet occupation'. The perceived threat of Moscow's imperialist ambitions supported the prevailing political discourse that Estonia was in need of 'extraordinary politics' (Lagerspetz and Vogt, 1998). The right-leaning Pro Patria party that took power in 1992 ran on the promise to 'clear the place' (Lieven, 1993, p. 285). In practice this resulted in dismantling the Soviet *nomenklatura* – including Russian-speaking Communist Party bureaucrats, enterprise managers, and collective farm directors – and appointing dissidents and Estonian émigrés to positions of power. This 'cleansing' was not limited to elites. By 1990 nearly 30 percent of the Estonian population was non-ethnic Estonian, owing to the Russification policies that resettled thousands of Russian speakers to The Baltics. A 1992 citizenship law granted automatic citizenship only to citizens or their descendants of Estonia's inter-war republic (1918–1940), effectively disenfranchising most ethnic Russians who had settled or were born in Estonia after Soviet annexation in 1940. The collapse of unprofitable state industries also had a disproportionate impact on Russian speakers who comprised a majority of the heavy industrial workforce in the northeast. In sum, the biggest 'losers' of transition – the Soviet *nomenklatura*, managers of uncompetitive industries, and Russian speakers – were effectively excluded from political competition.

The question arises why Estonia remained on this neo-liberal path after the initial 'shock therapy'. In other CEE states, we could observe during this period an alternation of strategies, with radical neo-liberal strategies followed by social liberal ones, and vice-versa (Orenstein, 2001). But Estonia's neo-liberal strategy remained more or less unchallenged. The 'cleaning' of Soviet *nomenklatura* and the disenfranchisement of Russian speakers are both crucial factors. But we can also point to the importance of ideas. The first Estonian Prime Minister Mart Laar of the Pro Patria Coalition party embarked on a 'big bang' program with ideological zeal after their strong showings in the 1992 elections. Laar famously declared that Milton Friedman's *Capitalism and Freedom* was the only book he had read, and declared Margaret Thatcher as a main inspiration (Laar, 2002; Bohle and Greskovits, 2012, p. 125). He appropriated the Nike slogan 'Just do it!' to launch his reform agenda. Concerning the question of how to pacify those who stood most to lose from liberalizing measures, Laar pronounced: 'Liberalize, then negotiate; but don't negotiate, then liberalize!' (Lieven, 1993, p. 89–90).

In just three years Laar's government had succeeded in abolishing all formal, and most informal, trade barriers. Laar recalls a moment when Estonia entered negotiations with the EU on a free trade agreement in 1994, suggesting that Estonia already had something to teach the far more protectionist-oriented EU:

> Visiting EU officials could not believe that any economy could possibly function without custom tariffs. It took a whole day before the officials had familiarized themselves with all the acts and regulations and convinced themselves that such a concept was really possible. (Laar, 2002)

Laar's expression of confidence reflects what Börzel, et al. (2010) refer to as 'obstinacy', or the challenging of the legitimacy of EU conditions – in this case to imposing external custom tariffs. Laar publishing his story of 'The Little Country that Could' for English-speaking audiences points more broadly to the importance he and other Estonian architects of transition placed on external recognition of their model. In the global economic rhetoric of identifying 'tiger' economies, Estonian leaders were pleased to be recognized, and promoted themselves, as a 'Baltic Tiger' or 'Nordic Singapore' (see Jansen, 2008). Laar was ultimately personally rewarded for his efforts by the Cato Institute, granting him the Milton Friedman Prize for Advancing Liberty in 2006. Justifying their choice, the selection committee writes, 'Laar has defied common wisdom in Europe to prove that economic freedom works' (Cato Institute, 2006).

Given this congruence of neo-liberal ideas and institutions, how did Estonian elites respond to EU demands once it entered EU accession negotiations in 1997? Given the high degree of domestic consensus around this path the impetus for change was almost exclusively externally driven (Dillon and Wycoff, 2002). Governing elites worked to fulfil the requirements of EU accession, and had the support of both ruling and opposition parties (Mikkel and Pridham, 2004). In the absence of significant party debate, technocratic intellectuals and think tanks played the most prominent role in opposing EU conditions. Editorials within the leading business daily *Äripaev* advocated delaying EU accession on the grounds that it would hinder Estonia's economic growth and competitiveness by forcing it to abandon its pro-market policies (Ehin, 2002). In a more populist vein, the 'No to the EU Movement' (or LEIEL in Estonian), a small, independently financed non-governmental organization, utilized Soviet imagery and comparisons between the EU and the previous regime in many of their materials. One LEIEL leaflet donned an image of the Soviet hammer and sickle in the middle of the European Union flag and lists 15 ways in which the USSR and the EU are alike, with the European Commission as Politburo and Europol the KGB. Uno Silberg, a professor of economics and leader of LEIEL, evoked such comparisons at the 30th Anniversary of the People's Movement against the EU in Denmark in 2002:

> The European Union is very like a disguised Soviet Union – a form of federal bureaucratic socialism. The advocates of Estonia's independence and sovereignty are against such a super-project. They regard it as downright harmful to the harmonious development of Estonia, Denmark and other European countries that aspire to maintain their national democracy and national independence. (Skov, 2005)

Silberg warns that 'The break-up of the old Soviet Union started from Estonia, and you can be certain that the European Union and its architects will not have an easy time either of trying to manipulate our country' (Lindstrom, 2014, p. 225).

As a long-time chairman of the parliamentary economic committee, Ivan Raig was one of the architects and most vocal proponents of Estonia's transition strategy – and later became one of the most prominent critics of EU accession. In Raig's (2003) account: 'We created a very liberal trade policy. My vision was Estonia as the Nordic Singapore. Membership of the EU will threaten us economically because we enter a market with many trade restrictions'. Raig pushed the government to apply for substantial transition periods upon EU accession, in order to maintain Estonia's 'attractiveness for foreign investors' and 'to preserve its business-friendly taxation system'. Heading up the accession preparatory committee in the parliament, Raig advocated that Estonia only harmonize its legislation to the minimum extent required. Raig also advocated bargaining for permanent derogations, and repeatedly cited Finland's success in negotiating a permanent derogation to preserve the duty-free status of the Åland Islands (Raig, 2003).

Failing to advance his agenda through official channels, Raig went on to found, with Igor Gräzin, the Euroskeptic think-tank Research Center Free Europe in Tallinn in 2003. Gräzin, a law professor at Tallin State University, suggests that the allegedly socialist – and expansionist – nature of the European project would weaken the Estonian economy. An advocate of unfettered free markets, Gräzin complains: 'To qualify for EU entry, we'll have to ditch the liberal market system that has made us so successful' (Skov, 2005, p. 1). Gräzin also criticizes the government's acquiescence to all EU demands. He states: 'Before jumping on this EU train, [politicians] haven't bothered to ask where it is going...or how much the ticket's going to cost. Even if it turns out to be cheap, it's not such a hot trip if the end of the line is an alligator infested swamp, now is it?' (Tarn, 2003, p. 1). Estimating that 'over 10 to 15 current EU governments are socialist-oriented', Gräzin says one of the reasons the EU has pressed Estonia to abandon its low-regulation, low-tax policies is that 'socialism is expansionist by nature. The European Union needs Estonia more than Estonia needs the EU' (Smith, 2001, p. 23).

In sum, Estonian EU-critics thus integrated two main critiques against the EU: that the sovereignty-constricting nature of the EU threatens Estonia's newly won sovereignty in general and Estonia's particular and successful neo-liberal variety of welfare capitalism in particular. Given the high degree of consensus around neo-liberal reforms – and the lack of resistance to these reforms by domestic interest groups or opposition parties – EU critics could portray EU pressures to deliberalize the Estonian economy by imposing protectionist barriers as a threat to a cohesive, as well as successful, national-development strategy. Elites most closely associated with Estonia's initial transition strategy became the most prominent EU critics. Instead of mobilizing opposition to the EU through formal political channels, Estonian critics utilized think tanks and media to promulgate positions critical of the EU. Moreover, they did not pursue these strategies in isolation. These Estonian critics also forged links with like-minded EU critics in the United Kingdom, and to a lesser extent Denmark, to advance their positions at the national and increasingly European-wide level.

Contesting the EU from the Left: the case of Slovenia

Slovenia's initial transition strategy differed significantly from that of Estonia's. They implemented a floating exchange rate, protected domestic industries through formal and informal trade barriers, subsidized national champions, and launched a privatization scheme that kept most ownership shares in domestic hands (see Bohle and Greskovits, 2012, pp. 182–222). To explain why Slovenia followed a less radical path of transition, one can point to Slovenia's favorable initial starting conditions. Like Estonia, Slovenia experienced recession and high inflation after gaining independence in 1991. But this recession period was shorter and less severe than in other CEE states. Slovenia lost important Yugoslav markets with the violent dissolution of SFRY, which comprised 60 percent of Slovenia's total exports. These losses were partially offset, however, by Slovenian firms' already well-established trade links with Western Europe, a legacy of Yugoslavia's liberal trading regime initiated in the 1970s.

Moreover, Slovenia inherited a significantly lower debt burden than other CEE states. While the SRFY was heavily indebted owing to massive borrowing in the 1980s, Slovenia negotiated a very favorable debt rehabilitation agreement with the IMF and international lenders after secession (Piroska, 2002). Taking on less than 20 percent of the total Yugoslav debt, Slovenia could manage repayment without much difficulty. While Serbia and Bosnia inherited a majority of resource intensive firms such as steel and heavy industries such as the unprofitable manufacturer of the Yugo, Slovenia inherited more competitive firms such as household appliance manufacturer Gorenje and pharmaceutical firm Kirka.

Relatively favorable initial starting conditions are undoubtedly a significant factor in shaping Slovenia's transition path. But one must also take into consideration elite decisions at this critical juncture. While Estonia was ruled by a continuous string of right-leaning governments, in Slovenia left-leaning coalitions led by the Liberal Democratic Party (LDS) ruled almost uninterrupted between 1992 and 2004 (Guardiancich, 2012, p. 381).

No 'cleansing' of former Yugoslav socialists occurred in Slovenia like it did in Estonia. Former socialist party members went on to assume prominent positions in government and industry. LDS governments pursued a strategy that entailed a substantial role for the state in the economic transformation and long-run development of the country. Slovenia's privatization policy favored domestic owners, entailing 40 percent of shares transferred to three state-controlled funds, 20 percent to employees, and the remaining 40 percent sold in public auction, with employees given a preferential rate. In practice, many 'voucher capitalists' chose to quickly sell their shares back to government funds, making the state and proto-state funds majority owners in many major firms by the mid-1990s.

Like in Estonia, the Slovenian government's overall reform strategy was supported by an early consensus among most party and technocratic intellectual elites. Unlike the case of Estonia, however, the Slovenian reform path was also shaped by the input of strong employer groups and trade unions, as well as their members. This consensus among social partners was institutionalized through corporatist bodies such as the National Council, a second parliamentary chamber representing local and functional interests. It was legally enforced through comprehensive bargaining agreements between labor and capital (Petrin, 1995). Slovenia's social welfare capitalist model was also inscribed in the Slovenian Constitution which defines Slovenia as a 'welfare state' (Article 2), and contains many elements of Slovenia's corporatist past, such as the rights of workers to make decisions (Article 75) (Lukšić, 1997, p. 9).

Slovenia's economic model also drew the attention of outside observers but for different reasons than Estonia. While Estonian leaders won accolades for exceeding the expectations of IMF proponents of liberalization, Slovenia went against the prevailing IMF wisdom. In 1992, Sachs traveled to Ljubljana to propose an alternative IMF-endorsed transition plan. Then Deputy Prime Minister Jože Mencinger and other Slovenian economists strongly opposed Sach's blueprint. Mencinger recalls, 'We listened to them, but didn't follow their advice. Their agenda was based on ideology, not economics. And the US advisors didn't see a difference between Slovenia and Mongolia' (Personal interview, 2006). When the government formally approved the IMF-endorsed plan, Mencinger submitted his resignation in protest. Prime Minister Alojz Peterle faced a choice: take Sach's advice and fire Mencinger, or listen to Mencinger and rebuff Sachs (Ganev, 2005, p. 360). The government ultimately passed a set of policies that diverged from the IMF proposed plan, including the voucher privatization plan. Mencinger went on to join the Board of Governors of the Slovenian Central Bank, where he pushed a macroeconomic policy agenda that also diverged from IMF advice. The Slovenian Central Bank chose a floating exchange rate in order to protect domestic industries and maintain a low current account deficit. Mencinger remarks that after the Czech financial crisis of 1999, his former IMF adversaries conceded that he might have been right, or 'at least not completely wrong' (personal interview, 2006).

When Slovenia entered formal EU accession negotiations in 1997, the Commission could now utilize active leverage over Slovenia's economic policies. One of the earliest and most contentious episodes in Slovenia's path to the EU occurred when the European Commission, at the behest of Italy, forced Slovenia to amend its Constitution in order to begin EU accession negotiations. The Commission demanded that Slovenia eliminate a clause that prohibited foreigners from buying Slovenian land (Bandelj, 2003, pp. 465–471). The Slovenian government complied, but not without prompting a heated parliamentary and public debate that raised concerns about the threat of EU membership to national interests (Bandelj, 2003, p. 379). Numerous other controversial issues followed throughout accession negotiations, such as opening telecommunications and insurance sectors to foreign competition or demands to close duty-free shops on the Austrian and Italian borders. Yet two of the most contentious issues became an opening for the state-owned Slovenian banking sector to foreign competition and the sale of a domestic brewery (see Lindstrom and Piroska, 2007).

After entering formal EU negotiations in 1998 and facing EU pressures to conform to conditions set out in the competition chapters of the *acquis*, the government formally complied by passing a 1999 Law on Banking that permitted foreign banks to open branches in Slovenia and abolished laws requiring equal domestic and foreign ownership shares in domestic banks. Nevertheless, by 2001 the government still owned nearly 90 percent of the banking sector. Finally yielding to mounting of formal and informal EU pressure, in May 2001 the Slovenian Government finally initiated a privatization plan for Slovenia's two largest banks, Nova Kreditna Banka Maribor (NKBM) and Nova Ljubljanska Banka (NLB). The privatization process signified one of the most economic policy changes in Slovenia since it gained independence a decade earlier and spurred considerable public debate. Although privatization of the banking sector in other CEE countries generated little public attention, in Slovenia a joint media campaign, public protest, and political opposition obstructed the privatization of Slovenia's second largest bank.

The European Commission, in its regular reports on Slovenia's progress towards meeting accession criteria, repeatedly raised the slow pace of bank privatization as a main concern and a sign more generally of the 'gradualist approach to structural reforms in Slovenia' (European Commission, 2003, p. 36). The Commission's 2003 'Comprehensive Monitoring Report on Slovenia's Preparations for Membership the European Commission' concludes: 'Although limited and partial privatization is taken place in the banking sector, the state remains strongly present in this sector while further privatization would promote reform conducive to competitiveness' (European Commission, 2003, p. 8). The initiation of formal talks with foreign bidders spurred heated public debate surrounding the NKBM privatization. In late October, the Maribor based 'Movement for People' sent a public letter to Finance Minister arguing that the sale of NKBM would not be profitable and would have negative effects on the Slovenian economy. The letter was followed by a well-publicized political and media campaign against the sale of NKBM, framed by the rallying cry 'Our Bank' (Lindstrom and Piroska, 2007, p. 122).

Technocratic intellectual elites figured prominently in public debate. Mencinger, along with other prominent Slovenian economists, argued against yielding to EU pressure to privatize the banks and open the sector to foreign competition. Among their arguments they pointed out the marked differences between existing EU member states, where a large percentage of banks were state owned and EU applicant states, where foreigner owners dominated the market. For instance, in 1997 the percentage of foreign-owned banks in EU members was less than 14 percent. In aspiring CEE states, in contrast, foreign-owned banks comprised over 75 percent of the banking sector, with Estonia leading at nearly 100 percent foreign ownership. Mencinger and Ribnikar argued that Slovenia had managed to avoid the fate of other post-socialist states by capitalizing on its initial strengths and opening it only slowly to foreign competition. They also framed their opposition to bank privatization in broader terms. In a 2002 editorial in the leading Slovenia daily, *Delo*, Mencinger writes: 'The demands by foreigners for an end to the Slovenian 'national-capitalism' are increasing, although I think that we have the right to defend our interests and our capitalism, since others also have that right' (Mencinger, 2003, quoted in Lindstrom and Piroska, 2007, p. 121). By the end of March 2002, almost a year after the government announced the privatization program, the government commission decided that none of the bidders who submitted binding bids met the privatization conditions and the bank remained in majority state ownership.

This ambivalence towards privatization and opening markets to foreign competition was most striking in the case of Slovenia's state-owned banking sector. But other industries were not immune to such conflicts. A battle between the Belgian-based Interbrew and the Slovenian brewer Pivovarna Laško over the takeover of the Ljubljana-based Pivovarna Union brewery, for example, was framed by local actors as a battle between David and Goliath: between a large EU-based conglomerate and a small, Slovenian national brewery. Indeed, Pivovarna Laško featured a quote from the 1940s hailing its independence from foreign influence: 'This is not a factory like those built with foreign capital, which came to engulf our land in slavery and misery' (Castle, 2012). The battle of the breweries – involving state agencies, foreign investors, local owners, the media, and the public – was fought during the most intensive stages of final EU accession negotiations (Lindstrom and Piroska, 2007, pp. 125-127).

The Slovenian beer market has long been dominated by two popular local brands: the Ljubljana-based Union brand, favored among Ljubljana connoisseurs, and the Maribor-based Laško, the favored brand outside of the capital. In November 2001 the Belgian-based brewing company Interbrew entered a bidding war with Laško for controlling shares in Union. Interbrew is well established in other parts of Central and Eastern Europe, having purchased local breweries in Bulgaria, the Czech Republic, Hungary, Romania, and elsewhere. While Interbrew's entry into other Central European markets raised little public attention, in Slovenia the proposed takeover prompted extensive domestic discussion. The so-called '"brewers" war' raised larger questions in Slovenia of whether privatization should be led by domestic or foreign capital. A multi-party coalition of over 30 members of the Slovenian Parliament petitioned to convene an emergency parliamentary session of the sale of Union to Interbrew. The campaign, led by Slovenian National Party Chairman Zmago Jelinčić, argued that it was in Slovenia's national interest to keep its best and most competitive companies in Slovenian hands. Borut Korun, leader of the Eurosceptic NGO who called the 23 December Movement, argued that foreign investors come to Slovenia merely for profit and that EU members skilfully use the relative poverty of the countries of the former Eastern bloc to their advantage (Slovenia Business Week, 2002a). The war culminated in a panel debate on the subject broadcast on national Slovenian television (Bandelj, 2003).

European officials weighed in on these debates about opening Slovenian markets to foreign investors. An EU official commented on the disputes by stating that 'foreign direct investment is undoubtedly positive for Slovenia's integration into the European economic arena' (Slovenia Business Week, 2002b). Spain's Ambassador to Slovenia remarked that Slovenia must 'find a balance between strengthening its own identity and opening outwards' (ibid.) Ultimately the sale of Pivovarna Laško to Interbrew fell through, leaving it in domestic hands when Slovenia entered the EU on 1 January 2004.

Concluding remarks

The chapter shows how throughout the EU accession process Slovenia was pressured to liberalize its economy, whereas Estonia was forced to deliberalize. Technocratic intellectual elites in both states resisted many EU pressures: Slovenian critics arguing that the EU is too liberal and Estonian critics suggesting it is not liberal enough. What they shared in common was an aim to preserve the nation status quo against the pressures of Europeanization. In many ways their aim was achieved. Slovenia entered the EU in 2004 having resisted EU pressure to privatize key industries and encourage further foreign investment. Estonia, on the other hand, imposed only the minimum necessary barriers to free trade and investment, but took on board few industrial or social policy goals (Bohle and Greskovits, 2012, pp. 133). That these two very different models of post-socialist welfare capitalisms persisted throughout very asymmetrical EU accession negotiations lends support to the claim that the EU project allows for welfare capitalist diversity (Scharpf, 2002). It also challenges the claims made by scholars of EU accession that EU conditionality would lead to convergence around one common set of EU rules and norms (Grabbe, 2003).

What can explain this high degree of continuity and consensus around each economic model? As discussed in Chapter 3, upon gaining independence in 1991, the main aim of each state was constructing and promoting an independent nation-state identity. Elites in both cases framed independence as 'returning to Europe' and leaving their respective decades-long histories as constituent republics of socialist federations behind. But this break was much more severe in Estonia than in Slovenia because of Estonia's different experience within the USSR. Slovenian elites could afford (in material and ideational terms) to maintain a stronger role for the state, including owning or protecting relatively competitive domestic firms, negotiating national collective bargaining agreements with strong labor unions, and maintaining generous social protections. Estonia, in contrast, exited with USSR with uncompetitive industries and weak civil society institutions. Thus socialist legacies are a key factor in explaining initial choices. But what can account for these choices remaining largely uncontested?

Size matters in that a consensus is generally easier to achieve in states with populations of around two million or less. Yet a crucial factor in explaining this high degree of consensus is that elites tied the economic model to national identities. In the case of Estonia, a 'nationalist contract' replaced a 'social contract' (Bohle and Greskovits, 2012, pp. 96–137). That is, as Kattel and Raudla (2013, p. 442) suggest, in the context of the Baltics 'what capitalism can deliver is not so much a socially more balanced society, but rather the survival of the nation'. Economic nationalism can also explain the equally high levels of continuity and consensus around the Slovenian model. Neo-liberal critics of Slovenia's model – including IMF officials, EU leaders, foreign investors, and domestic critics – could make little headway in opening the Slovenian market to more foreign investment. Protecting national industries, and their workers, was portrayed by Slovenia's architects of transition as protecting the Slovenian nation. The two cases demonstrate how economic nationalism is consistent with very different economic models (Helleiner and Pickel, 2005).

Many post-socialist governments try to promote economic agendas by appealing to the organic unity of the nation, but not all succeed. A final factor that can account for the 'obstinacy' of Estonian and Slovenian elites in the face of Europeanizing pressure is that their models were commonly perceived as a success. Returning to Ray, we can expect that the more favorably the public view their current national economic policies, the more opposed they will be to altering the status quo (Ray, 2004). This assumes a rational instrumental calculation of personal gain from such policies. But this assumption does not hold in Estonia which has some of the highest levels of inequality and rates of poverty among the eight post-socialist candidate states.

We can thus extend Ray's point to more ideational factors, namely how particular national variety of welfare capitalisms can become positively associated with sociocultural imaginings of the nation. Narratives that heralded Estonia as a 'Baltic Tiger' or highlighted the exceptional 'Slovenian way', propagated by internal and external actors alike, bolstered attachment to economic models that became seen as an important source of national prestige. This can go some way in explaining why each state resisted EU pressure to alter these models; when each model was heralded by external observers as successful, but according to very different criteria, they felt little need to change a good thing. Moreover, domestic critics of the EU could point to similar welfare capitalist models among old EU members, whether to the United Kingdom in the case of Estonia or Sweden in the case of Slovenia, to argue that diversity of models can coexist with European integration.

5
The Politics of Crisis (2007–2014)

Abstract: *The chapter examines the impact of the global financial crisis on the diversity of post-socialist welfare capitalist paths. It shows how global financial crisis in 2008 hit Estonia and Slovenia hard, prompting the most significant domestic debates over the appropriate role of the state since 1991. The crisis opened a window of opportunity for critics of each state's economic model to push for change: Estonian critics mobilizing for more active state intervention in the economy and Slovenian critics to push for further liberalization. The chapter finds that challenges to Estonia's neo-liberal model proved to be short-lived, with the crisis and entry into the Eurozone only solidifying Estonian elites' commitment to this path, whereas the Slovenian model has faced more significant challenges from above and below.*

Keywords: Austerity; banking crisis; Estonia; eurozone; fiscal crisis; protest; second-generation liberalizing reforms; Slovenia

Lindstrom, Nicole. *The Politics of Europeanization and Post-Socialist Transformations*. Basingstoke: Palgrave Macmillan, 2015. DOI: 10.1057/9781137352187.0006.

The previous chapter demonstrated that despite considerable top-down EU pressures during the accession process, we have observed more continuity than change in paradigmatic ideas underlying the two national welfare capitalist models – suggesting that the politics of EU accession has involved as much divergence as convergence in political economic norms. This chapter examines to what extent these divergent ideas endured once these states became full EU members. It suggests that in the period from 2004 to 2008 we witnessed more continuity than change. Estonia and Slovenia, like most post-socialist states, enjoyed high levels of growth, fueled by an increase in exports and, more importantly, an influx of foreign capital during the global economic boom years, which bolstered internal and external support of their particular welfare capitalist path.

It goes on to show how the global financial crisis in 2008 hit each state hard, prompting the most significant domestic debates in each state over the appropriate role of the state since gaining independence in 1991. I examine how these domestic debates were framed in the context of larger debates within the EU (and globally) over the most appropriate response to financial and fiscal crises. In both cases governments responded to demands by international institutions (namely the Commission and ECB) to pursue pro-cyclical monetary and fiscal policies, but differed in the extent to which they privileged these demands over competing domestic demands for more social, counter-cyclical measures. Both cases illustrate broader tensions in European democratic capitalism between the workings of European (and global) free markets and democratic (largely national) demands for social rights (Streeck, 2011). Each case demonstrates the former ultimately prevailing over the latter, but for different reasons and with different implications for the sustainability of their welfare capitalist models.

The enlarged EU and the economic boom (2004–2007)

After joining the EU in 2004, all new post-socialist states enjoyed a 'veritable boom period' (Jacoby, 2014, p. 52). Rates of growth in the period between 2002 and 2006 averaged six percent, considerably higher than the two percent growth rate average in the EU-15. The high growth rates in post-socialist states were fueled in part by exports, with most states doubling or tripling rates of exports to the EU during this period. High rates of growth can also be attributed to capital inflows. When global capital markets were awash in liquidity and looking for places to invest, new EU member states looked like a good bet. This was due in part to their newfound membership in the EU encouraging investor confidence (Bandelj, 2007; Drahokoupil, 2008). Many new EU member states had also embarked on sets of 'second-generation reforms' designed to make their states most attractive to capital investors (O'Dwyer and Kovalčik, 2007). One of the most publicized set of reforms was the 'flat tax' that spread across the region during this period (Appel and Orenstein, 2013). They also worked to limit costly regulations (within EU rules) and constrain wages by limiting the power of organized labor (Bohle and Greskovits, 2006).

These boom years coincided with the EU adjusting to its expansion from an EU-15 to an EU-25 comprised of an increasingly economically diverse set of states. Many observers feared that enlargement, by bringing in less economically developed and more neo-liberally oriented post-socialist members, would bolster the neo-liberal model at the expense of the European Social Model (Vaughan-Whitehead, 2003). They argued that given their lower wages and higher rates of unemployment, new member states threatened to put downward pressure on wages in the EU as a whole by western firms moving east and eastern workers moving west. They also pointed to 'second generation reforms' as exacerbating threats of competitive deregulation and 'social dumping' (Kvist, 2004). That is, in order to prevent capital from exiting to the East, critics feared the West European leaders would be motivated to slash corporate taxes, weaken state regulations, and constrain wages.

Tensions over social dumping erupted in a diplomatic imbroglio in 2005 when the then Finance Minister Nicolas Sarkozy remarked that if new member states could 'afford' a flat tax then they would not require financial help from the EU in the form of structural and cohesion funds. Adding fuel to the fire, just weeks after Sarkozy's outburst, George W. Bush arrived in Bratislava to praise Slovakia's flat tax as a 'model for Europe' (Lindstrom, 2010, p. 1310). German Chancellor Gerhard Schröder also criticized the new member states for taking aid from Brussels while reducing their tax rates to attract business from Western Europe, stating, 'It is certainly unreasonable that we finance an unbridled tax competition among each other via the budget of the European Union' (Stojaspal, 2004). Overall, with new EU member states enjoying rates of growth at least double and in some cases more than triple-old

EU members, fueled in part by second-generation liberalizing reforms, the idea that enlargement would lead to harmonious convergence was put under increasing strain in the immediate period following enlargement. But the 2007 financial crisis presented a host of new, far larger challenges to the enlarged EU.

The enlarged EU and the economic bust (2008–2014)

Most of the EU has faced a devastating period of recession since the collapse of Lehman Brothers in 2007 that triggered the worst financial crisis since the Great Depression. Many states faced severe banking crises, and most have witnessed a reduction or stagnation in rates of gross domestic output and rates of employment. All of the small open East European economies have been particularly vulnerable to financial crisis due to their reliance on exports and capital inflows. GDP growth rates (with the exception of Poland) declined dramatically between 2008 and 2009, with Latvia experiencing an 18 percent drop. As the financial crisis merged into a fiscal crisis, most new EU member states faced severe balance of payment problems. Latvia, Hungary, and Romania were forced to seek help from the IMF and the EU (see Lütz and Kranke, 2013; Jacoby, 2014). Expanding budget deficits and expanding government debt across the region made Euro adoption a more distant prospect for most new EU members from CEE, with the exceptions of Slovenia, which joined in 2007, Slovakia (in 2009), and later Estonia (in 2011).

A more in-depth account of the impact of the crisis on the EU and new member states is beyond the scope of this book. But we can make two observations relevant to our analysis of ideational conflicts in the EU. The first is that in the immediate period following the financial crisis, many observers argued that the crisis had undermined the neoliberal ideas that had become so dominant during the preceding boom years. With the European Commission proposing a host of new legislative measures to regulate hedge funds, credit-rating agencies, and other financial services industries, some argued that the balance was tipping towards the left-leaning, market-shaping position outlined in figure 1 (see Quaglia, 2010). The rise of movements such as Occupy and large public protests organized across the EU argued that the people (or the 99 percent) should not bear the burden for bailing out banks and investors (or the 1 percent). By 2011 observers were puzzling over the strange 'non-death' of neo-liberalism, an orthodoxy that appeared not only to have survived the crisis but emerged stronger than ever (Crouch, 2011). With the 'politics of permanent austerity' (Blyth, 2013) becoming common sense in Brussels, Frankfurt, and capitols across the EU, the kind of redistributive solidarity underlying the European (and national) social model is increasingly under threat.

The following sections examine how the economic crisis affected the continuity and consensus underlying the Estonian and Slovenian welfare capitalist models. In the boom years, each state became even more tightly integrated into the Single Market, with Estonia increasing its export growth between 2000 and 2008, by 165 percent and Slovenia by 199 percent (Jacoby, 2014, p. 55). Each state also experienced a rapid influx of foreign capital following their inclusion in the EU, although in Estonia most of this lending went to households and in Slovenia to state-owned banks and domestic firms. The 2008 financial crisis hit each state hard, with each experiencing the deepest period of recession since gaining independence in 1991. The chapter compares government interventions in each stage of the crisis, how these were debated and contested in each national public sphere, and their relationship to broader EU (and global) politics of crisis.

Estonia: neo-liberal politics as usual?

Estonia experienced one of the most dramatic declines in real GDP among all EU member states in the wake of the global financial crisis, suffering a 14 percent drop in GDP in 2009. Only neighboring Latvia fared worse. With Estonia enjoying annual growth rates of over eight percent throughout the boom years between 2000 and 2007, the bust was even more dramatic. Estonia's industrial output also suffered because of a fall in domestic demand and a squeeze in exports. By 2009 Estonia's industrial production dropped 34 percent, the most dramatic decline in the EU (Baltic Business News, 2009). At the same time Estonia's unemployment rate soared to 15.5 percent by the last quarter of 2009. By 2010, over 50 percent of Estonians reported that they were coping with some or great difficulty (Statistics Estonia, 2010). Estonia faced the most severe economic downturn in its post-1991 history.

At the start of the crisis, the Estonian government sought to deflect responsibility for its banking crisis by arguing that Estonia was an innocent bystander caught up in larger events. Estonian Finance Minister Jurgen Ligi remarked in a radio interview, for instance: 'What happened in Estonia was not a financial crisis, but a local bubble and its international impact' (Hõbemägi, 2010). The 'international impact' was namely Swedish banks exposed to a rapidly growing number of non-performing loans in Estonia and other Baltic States. Throughout the 2000s, Swedish banks, which comprised over 80 percent of the Estonian banking sector, provided Estonian with a steady stream of cheap credit (Bohle, 2013, p. 15). Like in neighboring Latvia, much of this influx of capital funded a housing and construction boom. When many of these loans became non-performing, the Swedish parent banks were forced to absorb the losses. As a result the Swedish Central Bank took out a precautionary loan of three billion euros from the European Central Bank to cover any potential bailout of its banks. That Estonian banks were almost completely foreign owned thus shielded the Estonian public sector from having to take on private financial sector liabilities, a fate that befell other states such as Iceland, the United Kingdom, and later Slovenia (Thorhallsson and Kattel, 2013, p. 86).

The Estonian government's main response to the growing fiscal crisis was a series of austerity packages centered on drastic cuts in public expenditures, including public sector wages, and tax increases. A number of external experts advocated the possibility of Estonia floating its currency, which had been pegged to the euro since 2001 (see Hugh, 2009). But this option received little serious consideration within Estonia. The government's steadfast commitment to fiscal retrenchment combined with a refusal to consider devaluing its currency made it a 'curious outlier' among developed states, most of whom were pursuing expansionist fiscal policies to mitigate the effects of crisis (Raudla and Kattel, 2011, p. 165). When deputy governor of the Bank of Estonia, Märten Ross, was asked about possible stimulus measures, he replied simply: 'The economy needs to adjust'. Similarly, when Minister of Economic Affairs, Juhan Parts, was queried on whether Estonia would 'betray' the 'laissez-faire philosophy of Milton Friedman' that guided their transition to date, he replied: 'We will stay a laissez-faire economy' (Dougherty, 2008). Indeed, the Estonian government never considered seriously interventionist or counter-cyclical policies to steer Estonia out of crisis.

The crisis did, however, open a window of opportunity for domestic actors to pose alternatives to the neo-liberal policy paradigm. The first real fissures in the government's austerity program appeared in May 2009 when Estonia's coalition government collapsed. Prime Minister Andrus Ansip ejected the Social Democrats from the coalition, including his popular finance minister, Ivari Padar. The Social Democrats had objected to cuts in unemployment benefits and pensions, and advocated across-the-board tax increases. The collapse weakened the ruling Reform party. Public opinion polls showed left-leaning parties making great gains at the Reform party's expense. In a June public opinion survey, just 15 percent of respondents expressing support for Ansip's party (Baltic News Service, 2010). The Reform Party went on to fare poorly in the June 2009 European Parliament elections. Having won 28 percent of the votes in 2004, it garnered just 15 percent five years later (Ehin and Solvak, 2012). The Reform Party's decline in support did not necessary result in gains for the opposition, however. The real winner of the EP elections was the independent candidate Indrek Tarand who won more than a quarter of all votes cast. A popular television host, Tarand became embroiled in controversy in 2005 when he was photographed at a football game wearing a t-shirt featuring prominent Estonian politicians under the slogan 'Kommarid ahju!' (Commies to the oven!) (Kurm, 2005).

Trade unions capitalized on fissures within the ruling coalition and growing popular discontent with the ruling party. The Estonian Trade Union Confederation (EAKL) called on the government to lower unemployment contributions, pay wages out of unemployment funds to avoid lay-offs, and increase the tax-free income threshold (Kallaste and Woolfson, 2013, p. 259). When the government continued on with its austerity measures, EAKL organized a strike in June 2009 in addition to a public demonstration front of the Estonian parliament (or Riigikogu). The Confederation invited members of the public to join the protest. Confederation Chairman Harri Taliga remarked that 'The Government's policy is clearly an attack against the weakest, so we are expecting everyone from students to pensioners' (The Baltic Course, 2009). Nearly 1800 workers from 15 enterprises took part in the strike, including 600 members of the Federation of Manufacturing Workers who picketed two factories on the Russian border. Lithuanian trade unions organized a solidarity action at the Estonian embassy in Vilnius in support of the Estonian trade unions.

Edgar Savisaar and the Center Party emerged as one of the most active and vocal critics of the government's austerity measures. In the October 2009 elections for Tallinn city council, Savisaar ran on a platform challenging the government's economic policy. Savisaar remarked: 'The Reform Party members imagine that the market regulates everything and there is no need for any economic policy... We are patching budget holes, not investing in the future' (Tere, 2009). Later he went on to declare that the 'only economic policy argument left to that government is that "it is even worse in Latvia"' (Baltic News Service, 2009b). Savisaar pursued an active campaign strategy that took the candidates out to the streets. In one campaign event, Savisaar handed out potatoes and firewood to people in need. In September 2009 a Centre Party-sponsored demonstration attracted over 1000 people, demonstrators held placards with phrases such as 'No to unemployment – yes to new jobs' and 'please do not cut pensions'. Counter-protesters also appeared, albeit in far fewer numbers. Evoking the common perception that the Center Party represents the interests of the Russian minority, one counter-protester carried a placard reading 'Edgar for mayor of Moscow' (Baltic News Service, 2009a). The counter-protesters capitalized on more general perceptions that protests against the government were fundamentally 'anti-Estonian' – a perception fostered by large-scale street protests by Russian speakers in 2007 against the removal of a statue in Tallinn commemorating Soviet soldiers from WWII, the largest demonstration in Estonia since 1980 (Thorhallsson and Kattel, 2013, p. 95; Ehala, 2009).

The Center Party went on to win a landslide victory in the Tallinn council elections. For the first time in Estonian politics, the two left-leaning parties – the Center Party and the Social Democratic Party – signed a coalition agreement. A Finnish columnist declared after the results that Estonia 'may no longer be a champion of a liberal economy' (Hõbemägi, 2009). Yet such a prognosis was premature. The Social Democratic Party has long been considered part of the so-called 'white forces' in Estonia, that is, non-populist, technocratic-style parties that span the political spectrum. In this respect, it shares as much or more in common with the technocratic Reform Party in style if not policy substance than the more overtly populist Center Party. Thorhallsson and Kattel (2013, p. 95) argue that the opposition as a whole was unable to capitalize on the deep social crisis and offer 'coherent alternatives' to the government's austerity programme.

The mobilization of trade unions and the center-left against the government's austerity agenda is significant insofar as it marked one of the first sustained challenges to the prevailing neo-liberal consensus. Yet the government's march to join the euro overshadowed any dissent. Despite facing a severe economic crisis, the Estonian government only redoubled its efforts to meet the Maastricht criteria for joining the euro by 2011. In the midst of the 2010 Greece crisis, and with growing fears of contagion, many observers were calling for a moratorium on all new euro adoption for several years. Yet with a debt to GDP ratio of just 9.6 percent and a budget deficit of 2.4 percent of GDP in 2010, Estonia not only met the accession criteria but also exceeded them by large margins. Instead of being viewed as a liability to the euro, many observers championed Estonia as a model for other states to follow. The chief economist for emerging market currencies at Barclays Capital, for example, remarked: 'Estonia seems pretty much a model of the fiscal discipline that the EU now wants to bring to the entire Euro area' (Tere, 2010). Prime Minister Ansip reinforced this image in foreign news outlets, commenting: 'We believe in conservative fiscal policy here in Estonia...despite all those painful budgetary cuts and tax increases' (EUBusiness, 2010).

The euro was far from overwhelmingly popular at home. But notably this opposition did not focus on the social repercussions of euro membership, but rather potential threats to national sovereignty and national identity. For example, a logistics worker from Tallinn, Peeter Proos, collected over 4000 signatures in on online petition objecting to the abandonment of the koon. He explained his motivation: 'Joining the Euro zone would be a grave threat to the economic independence of Estonia and will pull us back to the times of the Soviet Union, while we have all preconditions to be an independent European country like Switzerland' (Tere, 2010). In a press release, another campaigner, lawyer, and historian Anti Poolamets, made a case for Estonia not joining: 'For years, Estonia has conducted a principled fiscal policy – do not live beyond your means. As a result our country has the lowest government debt in Europe. Bailout projects in the Eurozone make Estonia's no-debt policy absurd – Estonians will have to pay the bills of banking machinations in other countries.' He went on to remark:

> I think that national currencies work better for the welfare of European countries because they better reflect the economic realities and differences therein. The 'one-size-fits all' ideology of the Eurozone is more of a reflection of the dreams of the European bureaucracy for a federal Europe than based on economic reasons...this is like the fulfillment of the dreams of the former Soviet hyper-centralist bureaucracy. (Proos, 2010)

On the eve of adopting the euro, the 'Save the Estonian Kroon' campaign lit candles across the country. Posters distributed to accompany the light display included one picturing the Titanic emitting clouds of smoke signifying Greece, Ireland, Portugal, and Spain. Above it declared: 'Estonia! Welcome to the Titanic!' (Proos, 2010). The press release also cited public opinion surveys reporting that 53 percent of respondents did not support the transition from the Estonian kroon to the euro.

In January 2011 Estonia become the third new member state, after Slovenia and Slovakia, to adopt the common currency. Having led Estonia in and through the crisis, the incumbent government led by the Andrus Ansip and the Reform Party went on to win 33 seats in the March 2011 elections. Touting its reputation as a good economic manager, the party campaigned on the slogan 'You can be sure' (EurActiv, 2011). Junior coalition partners Pro Patria and Res Republica Union took another 23 seats, giving the center-right coalition 56 seats of the 101-seat parliament. With a six seat gain from the last election, it appeared that the center-right suffered little fall-out from their austerity program. The European Parliament's European People's Party group chairman, Joseph Daul, praised the outcome: 'Estonia's rigorous reforms, budgetary balance and small debts during the recent economic crisis show an excellent example for the rest of Europe'. He went on to single out the junior coalition members. 'After gaining independence', Dahl stated, 'Estonia has developed into a role model for several European countries. Pro Patria and Res Public Union and its chairman Mart Laar have played a significant role in the process' (EurActiv, 2011).

While Estonia's austerity policies have been praised among certain economic and policy circles, it has also attracted a share rebuke from others. Paul Krugman serves as one notable example. In a post on his *The New York Times* blog 'The Conscience of a Liberal', he wrote a short critical piece entitled 'Estonian Rhapsody'. He first cited Estonia's newfound status as 'a poster child for austerity defenders', mocking their boosterism: 'They're on the Euro and they're booming!' He then went on to cite real GDP figures showing a 'terrible slump, followed by an incomplete recovery'. He concludes his post with the riposte 'this is what passes for economic triumph?' Estonian President Toomas Hendrik Ilves responded with a vitriolic Twitter post, accusing Krugman of being 'smug, overbearing and patronizing' towards East Europeans who choose to 're-elect governments that are responsible' (Keating, 2012).

Slovenia in crisis: the end of the Slovenian model?

Soon after Slovenia became an EU member in 2004, a new right-leaning coalition came to power, ending the 12-year reign of the LDS. The new government immediately launched an ambitious national restructuring program, with bank liberalization one of the key focus of reforms. In January 2005, Slovenian Prime Minister Janez Janša traveled to Estonia where he acknowledged that although Slovenia and Estonia took very different development paths, they now share the same views. Slovenia, he suggested, is 'facing the second wave of reforms, which Estonia has already implemented' (TV Slovenija 1, 2005). George W. Bush had notoriously mixed up Slovenia and Slovakia in 1999 when he remarked, 'The only thing I know about Slovakia is what I learned first-hand from your foreign minister, who came to Texas' (he had met the Prime Minister of Slovenia), prompting public outcry. Now Janša appeared quite happy for Slovenia to be associated with a country that offered one of the lowest levels of flat taxes and the most favorable policies to attract foreign capital.

The new government's ambitious reform agenda proved to be short-lived, however. The plans encountered significant resistance among trade unions and the public. One of the team of neo-liberal reformers, Jože Damijan, resigned in protest as head of the newly created Office for Development and Growth after just three months. Damijan reflected on the failed economic reforms, arguing that as the government and the public are 'socialist in mindset, to really change this mentality and liberalize the economy will take decades' (personal interview, 2006). Mencinger reflected on the failed reforms by saying that the government's reform proposals, like those of the EU's Lisbon Agenda on which it was based, with its 'abundance of empty words, newly invented phraseology and concepts, action plans and priorities, and similar claptraps' will go in to the dustbin of history as a 'worthless and harmless document' (Personal interview, 2006). In the next elections a left-leaning coalition resumed power, led by the former Yugoslav socialist party, the Social Democrats.

Meanwhile, like in the case of Estonia and other post-socialist states, during the global economic boom years, Slovenian state-owned banks had ready access to cheap credit. According to the NLB's chief executive, Janko Medja, this steady stream of credit flowing through Europe prior to the 2008 crisis encouraged banks like NLB to essentially give money away 'for free' (Bilefsky, 2013). Much of this money, like in other states, went towards funding a real estate, construction, and stock market boom. But in Slovenia it also went towards financing what Slovenians call 'tycoon loans'. In short, state-owned banks lent money under very favorable terms to Slovenian business insiders who, in turn, used the money to consolidate their ownership of firms. They also used this steady flow of credit to finance expansion into former-Yugoslav markets (see Svetličič and Rojec, 2003). The owners of Laško brewery, for example – the firm that had sworn off 'foreign capital, which came to engulf our land in slavery and misery' – now rushed to buy up majority stakes in Serbian and Bosnian breweries, as well as expand Laško's market share across former-Yugoslavia.

Up until 2007, therefore, the Slovenian model, based on active intervention of the state in the economy, remained more or less intact. But the global financial crisis following the collapse of Lehman Brothers in 2007 hit Slovenia hard. Between 2008 and 2009, Slovenia experienced a dramatic 8 percent fall in GDP (Statistical Office of the Republic of Slovenia, 2010). When housing and construction bubbles burst, domestic firms experienced a sharp decline in sales – both domestically and in important export markets of Western Europe and the Balkans. State-owned banks and firms that had enjoyed steady flows of cheap credit in the boom years after joining the EU and Eurozone now turned to the state for capital injections when the credit dried up. Government outflows towards recapitalization and increased social expenditure has placed significant pressure on the budget. With a public debt of 22 percent of GDP in 2008, one of the lowest in the Eurozone, by 2013 it had increased to nearly 63 percent (yet still below the 93 percent EU average) (Eurostat, 2014). By 2012 observers feared that Slovenia would be the next Eurozone country to seek an emergency bailout, potentially the first post-socialist euro state to do so. From being heralded as among the strongest new EU and Eurozone member states to now being considered one of its biggest problems, Slovenia has experienced a significant fall from grace.

The question arises to what extent the crisis has undermined the continuity and consensus underpinning the 'Slovenian way', or the exceptional neo-corporatist variety of post-socialist welfare capitalisms? The crisis indeed opened up a window of opportunity for advocates of the further liberalization of Slovenian political economy to push through policy reforms and austerity measures. But these efforts, by both left-leaning and then right-leaning governments, were thwarted by public referenda and political protest. Not until the threat of a bailout appeared to be a real possibility in early 2013 did the new government of Alenka Bratušek manage to pass a number of far-reaching reforms. But critics of the government's agenda argue that while it may have forestalled an immediate bailout, the government did it in a way that has undermined both the democratic legitimacy and societal consensus underpinning the Slovenian model.

When the new Social Democratic-led coalition came to power after the September 2008 elections, they quickly passed short-term measures in response to the worsening crisis. These included government investment in transportation projects, internet broadband, and cofinancing of other development-oriented investment projects. The new finance minister conceded, however, that 'Classic Keynesianism would have relatively little effect in a small open economy' (Escritt and Eddy, 2008, p. 27). Slovenian state-owned banks were also facing worsening balance sheets. Coming to the aid of its banks, the government passed a series of measures that injected fresh capital into banks, insurance companies, and pension funds, and created a loan guarantee fund. Government borrowing to assist the banks contributed to the rise of Slovenia's deficit to 5.5 percent of GDP in 2009, triggering the 'excessive deficit procedure' (Epstein, 2013, p. 543).

In response, in February 2010 the government proposed a three-year so-called 'exit strategy', a series of longer term measures and reforms to increase economic growth and competitiveness. It pledged to reduce public debt to below 40 percent of GDP, reduce the public sector by one percent a year, and sell shares in some state-owned enterprises (Slovenian Press Agency, 2010). The strategy included a 23 percent increase in the minimum wage, along with support for companies and redundant workers. But in March 2010, facing increasing deficits and corresponding pressure from the EU, the government unveiled a programme of structural reforms, including shortening layoff notice periods, lowering severance pay, increasing the minimum retirement age, and health sector rationalization (Stanojević and Klarić, 2013, p. 223). With respect to privatization, by 2010 the government had many enterprises from which they could choose. In addition to banks, state-controlled funds held stakes in companies as diverse as the grocery store chain Mercator (16 percent), Laško brewery (25 percent), white good manufacturer Gorenje (25 percent), pharmaceutical company Krka (25 percent), and a 50 percent in Telekom Slovenije (Stanovnik, 2011).

The prospective privatization deal that garnered the most attention was consistent with previous episodes in Slovenia's transition: Nova Ljubljanska Bank (NLB). When the government pledged to release a list of strategic assets that should remain state owned, the NLB was the first among those discussed. But significant disagreement existed among the Pahor government on this matter. The Finance Minister, Franc Križanič, opposed the sale of the banks. In an interview with the main business daily, *Finance*, the Prime Minister conceded that, 'Križanič deems state ownership of NLB to be in the national interest' (Sovdat and Urbas, 2010). Meanwhile, Development and European Affairs Minister Mitja Gaspari, who drew up the proposals, remarked that 'In this case, we should not talk about national interests, but about economic interests of our country, which are the only ones that matter now' (Štor, 2010).

The government's austerity measures were met with criticism across the political spectrum. The biggest opposition party, the Slovenian Democratic Party (SDS), argued that the government policies contradicted each other. They cited the rise in the minimum wage (increased by 22.9 percent in March 2010) that they passed while, at the same time, pledging to increase labor market flexibility. Employer associations voiced strong opposition to the minimum wage rise, whereas trade union officials spoke out against numerous proposals to increase labor market flexibility. Head of the largest trade union confederation Dušan Semolič, for example, warned: 'If the politicians go too far, we will stop them, with a referendum if necessary' (Štor, 2010). Semolič's threats were backed up by previous mobilizations of members. In autumn 2009 a wave of spontaneous strikes broke out across Slovenia, and the major trade union confederations organized a massive rally in Ljubljana (Stanojević and Klarić, 2013, p. 223). This time protests against the government's so-called exit strategy became violent. In May 2010 leading student organization held a protest outside the parliament, attracting over 15,000 people, which included a number of violent confrontations between protesters and the police.

The government carried on with the reforms unilaterally. But the trade unions and student groups had another tool at their disposal: the referendum. Students gathered over 40,000 signatures to trigger a referendum on the government's proposal to eliminate student jobs, which passed by large margins. Trade unions also organized a referendum on the government's structural reforms. In June 2011, Slovenians rejected the rise in the retirement age, by a 72 to 28 percent margin (Bryant, 2011). This was despite warnings by external observers that failing to reform the pension system would fail to control public debt and put Slovenia's credit rating in jeopardy. The IMF, for instance, warned that 'pension expenditure poses a challenge to fiscal sustainability' in Slovenia and that postponing pension and labor market reforms would 'lead to further deterioration in competitiveness and potential output growth' (Bryant, 2011). The pressures on Slovenia's budget continued apace. In

2011, the government spent almost a fifth of the total budget deficit on recapitalizing state-owned enterprises, as bad loans continued to accrue while the eurozone remained in recession. Yet fundamental features of the Slovenian model remained intact. As Stanjojević and Klarič (2013, p. 225) argue, 'all attempts at replacing social dialogue structures with unilateral "emergency" policies were basically unsuccessful'.

The crisis and the stalled reform agenda ultimately took its toll on the left-leaning coalition. In September 2011, the center-left government fell after a vote of no confidence. With the parliament failing to come to an agreement on a new leader, parliament was dissolved in October and President Danilo Turk called an early election in December – two events occurring for the first time in Slovenia's history. The December election was notable for the appearance of a host of new political parties on the Slovenian scene, including the ultimate winner, the center-left party Positive Slovenia. The new party was headed by Zoran Janković, mayor of Ljubljana and former president of the grocery store chain Mercator. When Janković failed to win the requisite number of votes to become Prime Minister, the task fell to the head of the party winning the second largest number of votes, the right-leaning SDS leader, Janez Janša. The early election was also notable in that LDS failed to win enough votes to take any seats in parliament – a dramatic reversal of their fortunes throughout the 1990s and early 2000s. Overall the early elections in almost all ways signified a remarkable departure from the largely stable electoral political scene since Slovenia gained independence (Guardiancich, 2012).

Once the center-right coalition was confirmed in February 2012, Janša set out far more radical austerity measures and structural reforms. Janša proposed to cut spending by 800 million euros in 2012, including the planned 15 percent reduction in public sector salaries and a gradual reduction of corporate income tax from 20 to 15 percent. In April trade unions organized one of the biggest public sector strikes in Slovenia's 20-year history. Ultimately the government compromised on the public sector pay cuts, scaling it back to around six percent. In exchange the unions signed an agreement with the government that enabled it to proceed with its reform agenda. Yet protest continued. In November 2012, 40,000 protesters gathered in Ljubljana. Demonstrators shouted 'We will not pay for your crisis' and hurled a large banner saying 'Enough' over the castle walls overlooking central Ljubljana. Dozens of smaller protests followed across the country. A December 2012 protest in Maribor turned violent as police helicopters fired tear gas to disperse over 10,000 protesters who demanded the resignation of the political elite, including the mayor of Maribor charged with corruption (Cain, 2012).

A notable feature of the protests is that they demanded more than a change of regime. They argued for 'the replacement of the entire political elite' (KOKS, et al., 2013). In an open letter, in English, distributed across the Internet, representatives of the protest wrote:

> Protesters blame this new recession not only on the autocratic, neo-liberal, corrupt and incompetent policies of the current government, but on a recent succession of corrupt self-serving governments... The dysfunctional legal system, the privatization of public funds, and hasty and extreme austerity measures has only aggravated the economic crisis, starving and destroying whole sectors of Slovenia's once healthy economy. To the dismay of its citizens, Slovenia is looking more and more like an autocratic neo-liberal banana state.

The letter cites recent polls to suggest that such demands have wide public support: 16 percent of the population taking part in demonstration, 67 percent supporting them, and 85 percent expecting demonstrations to continue.

The Janša government responded to the protests with a show of force, as well as rhetoric, with members of his cabinet referring to them as 'extremist left zombies' and 'radical neo-socialists' in the media. Janša also targeted elites opposed to his reforms. Condemning them as 'uncles behind the scenes' (or 'strici iz ozadja'), Janša argued that elites closely tied to the old regime were determined to obstruct change. Janša's reference to 'uncles' included elites in the media, higher education, culture, and some of the public sector. In response to the protesters' letter, the Slovenian Council of the Republic, a group of prominent public figures associated with the first Demos coalition, circulated an open letter of their own. After citing how its reform agenda has won external support from the European Commission and other organization, it concludes: 'The fundamental thesis remains: the process of Slovenian transition will have to be finished. This means de-monopolizing the state which is still largely owned by the old lobbies and rejecting the old undemocratic Communist beliefs and practices' (Slovenian Council, 2013). Ultimately Janša, facing corruption charges for arms deals made in his last term of office, lost the confidence of his coalition. His government fell in February 2013. Positive Slovenia nominated a relative political newcomer, Alenka Bratušek, to take over from party leader Janković who faced corruption charges of his own.

Bratušek inherited an economic crisis that was now making front page news across Europe. Following on the heels of the bailout of Cyprus, observers feared that Slovenia would become the sixth Eurozone country to seek a bailout. Attention focused on Slovenia's state-owned banks. By the time Bratušek took power, nearly 15 percent of the two largest state-owned banks were non-performing, constituting 6.8 billion euros, or one-fifth of its national economy (Bilefsky, 2013). This put Slovenia just below Greece, Ireland, and Hungary. It is worth noting, however, that Slovenia's banking system is relatively small by European standards: around 180 percent of banking assets to GDP, compared to, for example, 700 percent in Cyprus. With recapitalization expenditures pushing Slovenia's budget deficit and public debt levels well over Eurozone thresholds, the state sought to raise funds through the issuing of bonds, albeit with its ten-year bond yields close to seven percent.

The threat of a bailout reinvigorated advocates of radical reform measures. Bank privatization topped the list. For instance, the IMF concludes its statement of its staff visit to Slovenia in March 2013: 'Misconceived defense of "national interests", including the reluctance to sell assets to foreigners, burdens the budget and unduly prolongs the corporate and financial sector distress. A prominent privatization could convey a powerful signal to international investors' (IMF, 2013, p. 2). In addition to privatization, the IMF also supported the creation of a so-called 'bad bank', a sovereign holding company to take non-performing loans off bank balance sheets. While much of their focus was directed towards saving the ailing banking sector, the IMF also advocated a series of longer term structural reforms, including restructuring the pension system, increasing the flexibility of the labor market, and in general reducing the role of the state in the economy.

Bratušek's government followed many of the IMF's recommendations. A reform package announced in May 2013 included the creation of a bad bank (or the company for Management of Bank Claims), the privatization of state-owned companies, VAT increases, public sector pay cuts, among other measures. Initially proposed by the Janša government, the bad bank policy was widely unpopular. In mid-November 2012, the parliament agreed to back a referendum on the bad bank, requiring 40,000 signatures in 35 days for the motion to go ahead. Campaigners easily garnered enough signatures to make it obligatory. However, in December 2012 the Slovenian constitutional court ruled that a referendum on the proposed bad bank was unconstitutional. Although the court conceded that referenda were a constitutional right, it argued that a referendum on this matter would threaten other constitutional values, namely (a) the efficient functioning of the state apparatus necessary to ensure economic growth; and (b) the right to social security and free economic initiative (Žižek, 2013). The court's ruling was positively received by outside observers. The OECD, for instance, argues that 'boosting potential growth requires structural reforms, but the political economy of reform remains difficult, notably because it has been easy to use a referendum to veto a law' (OECD, 2013; p. 5). Žižek, on the other hand, used the case to argue that the crisis was becoming more a crisis of democracy than a financial crisis (Žižek, 2013).

Bratušek's center-left coalition government went on to prevent a bailout, shoring up Slovenia's troubled banks with 3.3 billion euros of state funds, and issuing bonds totaling 4.5 billion euros in 2014 (Novak and Irish, 2014). This coincided with other reform measures. For instance, after a heated plenary, the parliament agreed at the end of May, in a 78–8 vote, to modify the constitution to require a balanced government budget. Bratušek in her former role in the Finance Ministry had previously opposed such a plan, as had most of Social Democrats in her coalition. Yet in midst of bailout talks the measures passed handily. A vote on privatization was much closer. The government's privatization plan unveiled in May included the sale of 15 state-owned companies, including the second-largest bank, NKBM, and Telekom Slovenia. The government could choose to sell among over 100 companies it owns outright, or through its banks. Sale of the 'family silver' remains highly unpopular among Slovenians (Bandelj, 2008). Social Democrats, including its leader and agricultural minister Dejan Židan, remained vociferous critics of the plan, as well as the foreign minister and leader of the pensioner party (DeSus), Karl Erjavec.

A dramatic leadership battle within Positive Slovenia party led to resignation of Bratušek as party leader and prime minister in May 2014. The leadership contest was prompted by Janković seeking to resume control of the party amidst being under investigation for corruption. When Janković won the internal leadership contest, the coalition partners made good on their threat to dissolve the coalition. A new election was called for in July 2014. A newcomer to the political scene, Miro Cerar, topped the opinion polls leading his Party of Miro Cerar. A constitutional lawyer and son of a Slovenian Olympic gymnast and justice minister under the center-left Liberal Democratic Party, Cerar entered the race running on his novelty. 'I'm entering politics', Cerar explained, 'because I know that the situation in Slovenia is so bad that ... we need new people, new ideas, new practices' (Novak, 2014b).

Cerar's clearest policy position was to come out against the government's privatization process. 'Strategic firms, their infrastructure, should remain in the hands of the state', Cerar explained, listing in particular ports, airport, railways, and telecoms. With its leader beginning a two-year prison sentence, the right-leaning SDS party was running second. In the midst of the run-up to the election, Bratušek, who created her own party, called for a suspension of the privatization process. She denied the move had anything to do with the campaign, but that it was 'a responsible way to act with regard to state assets' (Norton, 2014). Cerar won the election by a wide margin, bringing in a new left-leaning coalition including the Social Democrats and the pensioner's party. Cerar nominated Bratušek for a European Commission post, which was later rejected.

Concluding remarks

The chapter demonstrated that while entry into the EU in 2004 did not significantly alter Estonian and Slovenian welfare capitalist models, the financial crisis in 2008 did present a critical juncture. The financial and fiscal crisis opened a window of opportunity for critics of each state's economic model, effectively sidelined for most of the previous two decades, to push for change: Estonian critics mobilizing for more active state intervention in the economy and Slovenian critics to push for further liberalization. The chapter finds that challenges to Estonia's neoliberal model proved to be short lived, with the crisis and entry into the Eurozone only solidifying both a material and ideational commitment to this path – despite radical austerity measures imposing significant social costs on its population (Sommers and Woolfson, 2014). The Slovenian model, on the other hand, has experienced more fundamental change. With the crisis exposing cronyism among government officials, state-owned banks, and domestic firms, the societal consensus that gave the Slovenian model legitimacy and sustainability has eroded significantly.

We can draw three sets of conclusions based on the above comparison of responses to the financial crisis in Estonia and Slovenia. The first concerns the role of societal actors in shaping government responses to crisis. While Slovenian trade union influence had seen a steady decline throughout the 2000s, they managed to constrain, if not prevent, the government from pursuing strict austerity measures in response to the crisis. Large-scale public protests and referenda against public sector cuts and labor market reforms contributed to the government pursuing a less radical and more gradual reform program. The Estonian government, in contrast, faced little sustained social unrest or concerted public opposition to its radical austerity measures. The mobilization of Estonian trade unions is significant in that it was a rare display of public protest against neo-liberal policies. However, as Kallaste and Woolfson (2013, p. 26) suggest, 'substantive social dialogue has been almost completely ignored in Estonia, with the government unilaterally pursuing its austerity policies'. The right-leaning government, in power since the crisis, has enjoyed record high approval ratings, despite austerity measures having imposed high costs across Estonian society.

The chapter also demonstrates how external pressure from international institutions (namely the European Commission and European Central Bank, but also the IMF and OECD) and international markets were received differently depending on collective ideas underpinning each welfare capitalist model. In Estonia, the government's response to crisis was clear: 'we cannot abandon the peg; we have to adopt the euro; we therefore have to adjust the budget' (Kattel and Raudla, 2013, p. 441). But this program in many ways went against prevailing wisdom at the time, not least from some in the IMF who advocated easing deficit targets, devaluating currencies, delaying Euro adoption, and using greater 'revenue measures' to steer the country out of crisis (Lütz and Kranke, 2013, p. 11). As Thorhallsson and Kattel (2003, p. 86) suggest, Estonian elites rejected such ideas not out of principle; stimulus measures remained 'alien' in Estonia as two decades of neo-liberal programs had 'hallowed out the political and bureaucratic arena of both ideas and competencies'. Estonian leaders continued on their radical austerity path to the euro largely unchallenged from above or below.

In Slovenia, the government faced pressure from international institutions to reduce the role of the state in the economy. This advice was embraced by domestic elites who had been thwarted in their attempts to change Slovenia's course throughout the 1990s and early 2000s. But in contrast to Estonia, Slovenian elites pursued a far less radical agenda, constrained by popular dissent, expressed both through the ballot box and in the streets. The threat of a bailout and pressure from international markets ultimately prompted more radical reforms. But the chapter shows that the implementation of such reforms required blocking democratic channels, notably public referenda (a move that had long been advocated by international institutions), and resorting in some cases to force to suppress public protests. The new left-leaning Slovenian government formed in September 2014 now finds itself facing a dilemma familiar to leaders of Greece, Ireland, Spain, and other states, namely:

> How far [they] can go in imposing the property rights and profit expectations of the markets on their citizens, while avoiding having to declare bankruptcy and protecting what may still remain of their democratic legitimacy. (Streeck, 2011, p. 24)

Finally, that Estonia emerged from the crisis to serve once again as a 'success story' for neo-liberal champions within and beyond the EU, while the 'Slovenian way' has experienced a significant fall from grace, reflects larger trends in the European (and global) political economy. For one, it suggests that the diversity of post-socialist welfare capitalism may be diminishing post crisis, with states converging towards the Baltic model due to the constraints of both the euro and international markets. The second is that by 2014 the divisions within Europe appear starker than did a decade ago when these countries joined. The idea that EU (or euro) membership would lead to convergence has been seriously undermined, not only in post-socialist states but also around the periphery of Europe. Streeck (2011, p. 28) suggests class conflicts have been translated into international conflicts, 'pitting against each other nations that are each subject to the same financial market pressures for public austerity.' The idea that the European Social Model could provide a redistributive, solidaristic, *European* counter-movement to market-making forces seems more elusive, while demands to protect national liberal and social market economies strengthen.

6
Conclusions

Abstract: *The concluding chapter outlines two main contributions and areas for future research. The first is that different welfare capitalist trajectories are inscribed with different kinds of social meanings, giving rise to different responses to common EU pressures. Further work remains in analyzing the inter-subjective social foundations on which such narratives rely and how and when social understandings can change. A second conclusion is that post-socialist elites engage more in the defense of the national status quo than shaping the European project. Preliminary research suggests that Estonian elites have been more proactive in pushing for a right-leaning, market-making EU than Slovenians have advocated for a more 'Social Europe'. Further research is required to understand when and how domestic politics of Europeanization are waged at the European level.*

Keywords: Constructivist political economy; democratic capitalism; discursive institutionalism; economic nationalism; the future of Social Europe

Lindstrom, Nicole. *The Politics of Europeanization and Post-Socialist Transformations*. Basingstoke: Palgrave Macmillan, 2015. DOI: 10.1057/9781137352187.0007.

The main conclusion of the book is that ideas underlying different types of national capitalist welfare models shape domestic political conflicts over Europeanization in the new member states of CEE as they do in Western Europe. In particular, it has shown how the architects of particular transformation paths have contested EU pressures on the grounds that they threaten historical and cultural values underlying their particular economic nation. Yet they ascribe these external EU pressures with different meanings, in some cases for being too liberal and in other cases not liberal enough. The principle they share is preserving the status, whether a 'national social model' or 'national liberal market model' (see Figure 2.1), against, further integration at the European level.

The extent to which particular CEE elites are likely to contest EU pressures depend on a number of factors. The first relevant factor is the degree of continuity and consensus underlying transformation paths. In cases where we witness more regime instability than in Estonia and Slovenia, or where the 'status quo' is subject to more change, we can expect less cohesive positions on the EU. Moreover, we can expect more attachment to the status quo the more that economic transformation paths are construed as integral to national identities. While 'economic nations' can be constructed around different economic policies, the salience of such identities lies in their nationalist content. Finally, we can expect more resistance to EU-induced change the more a particular economic model is perceived (internally and externally) as a 'success'. Thus for states like Romania or Bulgaria that lag behind the EU along many indicators, *any* change is likely to be perceived as preferable to the status quo (Krastev, 2013).

The book makes a number of broader contributions to our understanding of the role of ideas in comparative political economy. For one, it sheds light on the importance of ideas in shaping different post-socialist transformation paths. More material or structural accounts would argue that Estonia pursued a more radical reform agenda because it had no choice and that Slovenia pursued a more gradualist one because it could afford to. But this does not explain why there was such a high degree of consensus and continuity around each particular path. The ideational approach presented here suggests that at the critical juncture of the break-up of federal socialist states, transition elites construed economic strategies as key to the very survival, as well as future prosperity, of the nation. By focusing on 'architects of transition' as key agents in generating and diffusing such ideas (see Hall, 1993, pp. 280–281), it addresses criticisms of ideational approaches for neglecting the role of agency (Lieberman, 2002, p. 700). It also addresses criticisms of varieties of welfare capitalism frameworks for presenting economic models as static, functional, ideal types by showing how political actors endow different economies in which they are embedded with social purpose and how this purpose is subject to debate and change (see Abdelal, Blyth, and Parsons, 2010, p. 9).

A second contribution of the book to constructivist approaches to comparative political economy is demonstrating how ideas matter in shaping domestic responses to common external pressures. Many comparative political economy accounts of Europeanization treat EU pressures as an exogenous source of change, directly or indirectly eroding European national social welfare states and shaping candidate countries in its own image (Jackson and Deeg, 2008, p. 702). A more endogenous account of change focuses our attention on how 'Europe' and the 'EU' are moving targets. If we understand the EU as an open-ended and contested project, we can then assess and compare the ideas political elites hold about the EU among the many narratives and understandings that comprise the 'ideational context' of European integration (Hay and Rosamond, 2002, p. 151; Jabko, 2006; Parsons, 2003). Doing so can help us better understand how particular frames shape domestic conflicts over the infiltration of EU rules and norms into the domestic sphere (the 'Europeanization dimension'). It can also help us ascertain their positions on distributional conflicts within the EU (the 'functional dimension').

The book concludes with two areas for future research. The first concerns how to disentangle the inter-subjective understandings that underlie different capitalist welfare states and the discursive strategies deployed by elites to formulate and legitimate particular courses of action (see Cox, 2001; Hay and Rosamond, 2002; Schmidt, 2010; Berman, 2013). This analysis follows the kind of two-step disursive institutionalist approach advocated by Schmidt (2006; 2010). I start with national welfare capitalist categories derived from historical institutionalist approaches, then use discursive approaches to show how these political economic different trajectories are inscribed with social meanings and give rise to different responses to common EU pressures. Yet further work remains in analyzing the more inter-subjective 'social tissue' (Polanyi, 1944) underlying elite discursive strategies. These strategies are dependent on elite discourse resonating with collectively held ideas, but it is much harder to identify these ideas when 'no one utters them' (Béland and Cox, 2011, p. 13). We must also explore further under what conditions these 'ties that bind' unravel.

A second area for future research is to assess to what extent new member states such as Estonia and Slovenia have become more proactive than reactive in their relationship with the EU. I have shown in this book how elites in each state engaged more in 'rear guard action in defense of the national interest' rather than 'engagement in the co-authorship of a European project' (Hay and Rosamond, 2002, p. 159). In other work I have suggested that Estonian governing elites have been far more active than their Slovenian counterparts in pushing for a particular idea of the European project, in Estonia's case one based on neoliberal principles (Lindstrom, 2011). But this exposes a limitation with a focus on national elites. With citizens across the EU viewing their states as increasingly unresponsive to their needs and demands, we may see the strengthening of transnational political mobilization. CEE advocates of neo-liberal reforms have, to date, been far more successful organizing transnationally than their critics (Appel and Orenstein, 2013). But the crisis may open new windows of opportunity for citizens across the EU-28 to engage in a co-authorship of a European project that seeks to reinvigorate an embattled European Social Model. This 'functional dimension' of political contention in the EU over its underlying social purpose, degree of institutionalization, and future trajectory is even more vital in the wake of crisis. We can thus explore how the crisis of democratic capitalism (Streeck, 2011) may strengthen other forms of organizing and protest beyond the state, which a growing number of citizens view as increasingly unresponsive and illegitimate.

References

Aalto, P. (2000), 'The saviour and other Europes: identity, interests and geopolitical images of Europe in Estonia', *Paper presented at International Studies Association, Los Angeles*, 14–18 March.

Aalto, P. (2003), 'Revisiting the security/identity puzzle in Russo-Estonian relations', *Journal of Peace Research* 40, pp. 573–591.

Abdelal, R. (2001), *National Purpose in the World Economy: Post-Soviet States in Comparative Perspective* (Ithaca: Cornell University Press).

Abdelal, R. (2005), 'Nationalism and International Political Economy in Eurasia', in Helleiner, E. and Pickel, A. (eds) *Economic Nationalism in a Globalizing World* (Ithaca: Cornell University Press).

Abdelal, R., Blyth M. and Parsons C., (eds) (2010), *Constructing the International Economy.* (Ithaca: Cornell University Press).

Adam, F., Kristan, P. and Tomšič, M. (2009), 'Varieties of capitalism in Eastern Europe (with special emphasis on Estonia and Slovenia)', *Communist and Post-Communist Studies* 42, pp. 65–81.

Appel, H. and Orenstein, M. (2013), 'Ideas versus resources: explaining the flat tax and pension privatization revolutions in Eastern Europe and the former Soviet Union', *Comparative Political Studies* 46, pp. 123–152.

Ash, T. G. (1990), *The Uses of Adversity: Essays on the Fate of Central Europe* (New York: Vintage Books).

Bakić-Hayden, M. (1995), 'Nesting orientalisms: the case of former Yugoslavia', *Slavic Review* 54, pp. 917–931.

Baltic Business News (2009), 'Estonian industrial production fell most in EU', 12 June.

Baltic News Service (2009a), 'Estonia: center party rally passes without incident', 24 September.

Baltic News Service (2009b), 'Estonian centrist leader flings severe criticism at reform party, coalition' 14 November.

Baltic News Service (2009), 'Estonians see trade unions as weak', 7 December.

Baltic News Service (2010), 'Estonian reform party backed by 21 per cent of voters in June', 10 July.

Bandelj, N. (2003), 'Particularizing the global: reception of foreign direct investment in Slovenia', *Current Sociology* 51, pp. 377–394.

Bandelj, N. (2004), 'Negotiating global, regional, and national forces: foreign investment in Slovenia', *East European Politics and Societies* 18, pp. 455–480.

Bandelj, N. (2007), *From Communists to Foreign Capitalists: The Social Foundations of Foreign Investment in Post-Socialist Europe* (Princeton, NJ: Princeton University Press).

Bandelj, N. (2008), 'Economic objects as cultural objects: discourse on foreign investment in post-socialist Europe', *Socio-Economic Review* 6, pp. 671–702.

Béland, D. and Cox R. H. (eds) (2011), *Ideas and Politics in Social Science Research* (Oxford: Oxford University Press).

Berman, S. (2013), 'Ideational theorizing in the social sciences since "policy paradigms, social learning, and the state', *Governance* 26, pp. 217–237.

Bilefsky, D. (2013), 'Slovenia falls from economic grace, struggling to avert a bailout', *The New York Times* 5 May.

Blyth, M. (1997), ' "Any more bright ideas?' The ideational turn in comparative political economy', *Comparative Politics* 29, pp. 229–250.

Blyth, M. (2002), *Great Transformations: Economic Ideas and Institutional Change in the Twentieth Century* (New York: Cambridge University Press).

Blyth, M. (2013), *Austerity: The History of a Dangerous Idea* (Oxford: Oxford University Press).

Bohle, D. (2013), 'Post-socialist housing meetings transnational finance: foreign banks, mortgage lending, and the privatization of welfare in Hungary and Estonia', *Review of International Political Economy* 21, pp. 913–948.

Bohle, D. and Greskovits B. (2006), 'Capitalism without compromise: strong business and weak labor in Eastern Europe's new transitional industries', *Studies in Comparative International Development* 41, pp. 3–25.

Bohle, D. and Greskovits B. (2007), 'Neoliberalism, embedded neoliberalism, and neo-corporatism: towards transnational capitalism in Central-Eastern Europe', *West European Politics* 30, pp. 443–466.

Bohle, D. and Greskovits B. (2012), *Capitalist Diversity on Europe's Periphery* (Ithaca: Cornell University Press).

Börzel, T., Hofmann T., Panke D., Sprungk C. (2010), 'Obstinate and inefficient: why member states do not comply with European law', *Comparative Political Studies* 43, pp. 1363–1390.

Böhmelt, T. and Freyburg T. (2014), 'Diffusion of compliance in the "race towards Brussels?" A spatial approach to EU accession conditionality', *West European Politics*, http://dx.doi.org/10.1080/01402 382.2014.943523.

Börzel, T. (2011), 'When Europe hits...beyond its borders: Europeanization and the near abroad', *Comparative European Politics* 9, pp. 394–413.

Breen, S. (2013), 'Nostra culpa', *Independent* blog. http://blogs.independent.co.uk/2013/04/12/nostra-culpa-the-blog-the-estonian-presidents-twitter-rant-and-the-resulting-libretto/, date accessed 15 July 2013.

Brinegar, A. P., Jolly S. K., and Kitschelt H. (2004), 'Varieties of Capitalism and Political Divides over European Integration', in Marks G. and Steenbergen M. (eds) *European Integration and Political Conflict* (Cambridge: Cambridge University Press).

Bruszt, L. (2002), 'Making markets and Eastern enlargement: diverging convergence?', *West European Politics* 25, pp. 121–140.

Bryant, C. (2011), 'Slovenia rejects pension reform', *Financial Times*, 5 June.

Buckley, N. (2013), 'Slovenia finally embarks on privatisations', *The Financial Times*, 20 June.

Buchen, C. (2007), 'Estonia and Slovenia as Antipodes', in Lane, D. and Myant, M. (eds) *Varieties of Capitalism in Post-Communist Countries* (Palgrave Macmillan).

Bunce, V. (1999), 'The political economy of post-socialism', *Slavic Review* 58, pp. 756–793.

Cain, P. (2012), 'Why Slovenia is content no more', *BBC News*, 4 December.

Castle, S. (2012), 'Slovenia encounters debt trouble and may need bailout', *The New York Times*, 14 September.

Cato Institute (2006), 'Mart Laar: winner of the 2006 Milton Friedman Prize', http://www.cato.org/friedman-prize/mart-laar, date accessed 17 July 2008.

Chirot, D. (1999), 'Who is western, who is not, and who cares?', *East European Politics and Societies* 13, pp. 244–248.

Clift, B. and Woll, C. (2012), 'Economic patriotism: reinventing control over open markets', *Journal of European Public Policy* 19, pp. 307–323.

Connolly, W. (2002), *Identity/Difference: Democratic Negotiations of a Political Paradox*, expanded edition (Ithaca, NY: Cornell University Press).

Copeland, P. (2012), EU enlargement, the clash of capitalisms and the European social model', *Comparative European Politics* 10, pp. 476–504.

Cowles, M. G., Caporaso J. and Risse-Kappen T. (eds) (2001) *Transforming Europe: Europeanization and Domestic Change* (Ithaca: Cornell University Press).

Cox, R. H. (2001), 'The social construction of an imperative: why welfare reform happened in Denmark and the Netherlands but not in Germany', *World Politics* 53, pp. 463–498.

Chwieroth, J. (2010), 'Shrinking the State: Neoliberal Economists and Social Spending in Latin America', in Abdelal R., Blyth M. and Parsons C. (eds) *Constructing the International Economy* (Ithaca: Cornell University Press).

Crane, G.T. (1998), 'Economic nationalism: bringing the nation back in', *Millenium* 27, pp. 55–75.

Crouch, C. (2011), *The Strange Non-Death of Neo-Liberalism* (Cambridge: Polity).

De Vilde, P. and Trenz, H. (2012), 'Denouncing European integration: euroskepticism as polity contestation', *European Journal of Social Theory* 15, pp. 537–554.

Debeljak, A. (1994), *Twilight of the Idols: Recollections of a Lost Yugoslavia* (Buffalo, NY: White Pine Press).

Dillon, D. and Wycoff, F. (2002), *Creating Capitalism: Transition and Growth in Post-Soviet Europe* (Cheltenham: Edward Elgar).

Dougherty, C. (2008), 'Estonia's let-it-be economy is rattled by worldwide distress', *The New York Times*, 10 October.

Drahokoupil, J. (2008), *Globalization and the State in Central and Eastern Europe: The Politics of Foreign Direct Investment* (London: Routledge).

Ehala, M. (2009), 'The bronze soldier: identity threat and maintenance in Estonia', *Journal of Baltic Studies* 40, pp. 139–158.

Ehin, P. (2002), 'Estonian euroskepticism: a reflection of domestic politics?', *East European Constitutional Review* 11, pp. 96–106.

Ehin, P. and Solvak, M. (2012), 'Party voters gone astray: explaining independent candidate success in the 2009 European elections in Estonia', *Journal of Elections, Public Opinion and Parties* 22, pp. 269–291.

Esping-Andersen, G. (1990), *The Three Worlds of Welfare Capitalism* (Cambridge: Polity).

Epstein, R. (2006), 'Cultivating consensus and creating conflict international institutions and the (de)politicization of economic policy in postcommunist Europe', *Comparative Political Studies* 39, pp. 1019–1042.

Epstein, R. (2013), 'Central and East European bank responses to the financial "crisis": do domestic banks perform better in a crisis than their foreign-owned counterparts?', *Europe-Asia Studies* 65, pp. 528–547.

Escritt, T. and K. Eddy (2008), 'Downturn fails to dent self-sufficient spirit', *Financial Times*, 10 December.

EUBusiness (2010), 'As Eurozone crisis bites, newcomer Estonia urges austerity', 16 June.

EurActiv (2011), 'Estonia's ruling center-right coalition wins election', 7 March.

European Commission (2004), 'Comprehensive monitoring report of Slovenia's preparation for membership', Brussels.

European Commission (2003), *Comprehensive Monitoring Report on Slovenia's Preparation for Membership* (Brussels: European Commission).

Eyal, G; Szelényi I. and Townsley E. (1998), *Making Capitalism without Capitalists: The New Ruling Elites in Eastern Europe* (New York: Verso).

Falkner, G. and O. Treib (2008), 'Three worlds of compliance or four? The EU-15 compared to new member states', *Journal of Common Market Studies* 46, pp. 293–313.

Feldman, M. (2001), 'European integration and the discourse of national identity in Estonia', *National Identities* 3, 1, pp. 5–21.

Feldmann, M. (2007), 'Emerging varieties of capitalism in transition countries: industrial relations and wage bargaining in Estonia and Slovenia', *Comparative Political Studies* 39, pp. 829–854.

Feldmann, M. and Sally R. (2002), 'From the Soviet Union to the European Union: Estonian trade policy, 1991–2000', *The World Economy* 25, pp. 79–106.

Fougner, T. (2006), 'Economic nationalism and maritime policy in Norway', *Cooperation and Conflict* 41, pp. 177–201.

Gabel, M. (1998), *Integration and Interests: Market Liberalization, Public Opinion and the European Union* (Ann Arbor: University of Michigan Press).

Gal, S. (1991), 'Bartók's funeral: representations of Europe in Hungarian political rhetoric', *American Ethnologist* 81, pp. 440–458.

Ganev, V. (2005), 'The "triumph of neoliberalism" reconsidered: critical remarks on ideas-centered analyzes of political and economic change in post-communism', *East European Politics and Societies* 19, pp. 343–378.

Gilpin, R. (1987), *The Political Economy of International Relations* (Princeton: Princeton University Press).

Gourevitch, P. (1978), 'The second image reversed: international sources of domestic politics', *International Organization* 32, pp. 881–912.

Grabbe, H. (2003), 'Europeanization Goes East: Power and Uncertainty in the EU Accession Process' in Featherstone K. and Radaelli C. (eds) *The Politics of Europeanization* (Oxford: Oxford University Press).

Guardiancich, I. (2012), 'The uncertain future of slovenian exceptionalism', *East European Politics and Societies* 26, pp. 380–399.

Haavisto, T. (1997), *The Transition to a Market Economy: Transformation and Reform in the Baltic States* (London: Edward Elgar).

Halikiopoulou, D., Nanou K., and Vasilopoulou S. (2012), 'The paradox of nationalism: the common denominator of radical right and radical left euroscepticism', *European Journal of Political Research* 51, pp. 504–539.

Hall, P. (1993), 'Policy paradigms, social learning and the state: the case of economic policy making in Britain', *Comparative Politics* 25, pp. 275–296.

Hansen, L. (1996), 'Slovenian identity: state-building on the Balkan border', *Alternatives* 21, pp. 473–496.

Havel, V. (1990), 'President Václav Havel's speech to the Polish Sejm and senate, January 21, 1990' *East European Reporter* 4, pp. 55–57.

Hay, C. and Rosamond B. (2002), 'Globalization, European integration, and the discursive construction of economic imperatives', *Journal of European Public Policy* 9, pp. 147–167.

Helleiner, E. (1994), 'Economic nationalism as a challenge to neoliberalism? Lessons from the 19th century', *International Studies Quarterly* 46, pp. 307–329.

Helleiner, E. and Pickel A. (eds) (2005), *Economic Nationalism in a Globalizing World* (Ithaca: Cornell University Press).

Hellman, J. (1998), 'Winners take all: the politics of partial reform in postcommunist transitions', *World Politics* 50, pp. 203–234.

Hille, P. and Knill C. (2006), 'It's the bureaucracy, stupid: the implementation of the acquis communitaire in EU candidate countries, 1999–2003', *European Union Politics* 7, pp. 531–552.

Hix, S. (1999), 'Dimensions and alignments in European union politics: cognitive constraints and partisan responses', *European Journal of Political Research* 35, pp. 69–106.

Hix, S. and Goetz K. (2000), 'Introduction: European integration and national political systems', *West European Politics* 23, pp. 1–8.

Hix, S., Noury A. and Roland G. (2007), *Democratic Politics in the European Parliament* (Cambridge: Cambridge University Press).

Hõbemägi, T. (2009) 'Columnist: Estonia no longer a champion of liberal economy', *Baltic Business News*, 21 October.

Hooghe, L. and Marks G. (1999), 'The Making of a Polity: The Struggle over European Integration', in Kitschelt H., Lange P., Marks G. and Stephens J. (eds) *Continuity and Change in Contemporary Capitalism* (Cambridge: Cambridge University Press).

Hooghe, L. and Marks G. (2008), 'A postfunctionalist theory of European integration: from permissive consensus to constraining dissensus', *British Journal of Political Science* 39, pp. 1–23.

Hooghe, L., Marks G. and Wilson C. (2002), 'Does left/right structure party positions on European integration?', *Comparative Political Studies* 35, pp. 965–989.

Höpner, M. and A. Shäfer (2012), 'Embeddedness and regional integration: waiting for Polanyi in a hayekian setting', *International Organization* 66, pp. 429–455.

Huang, M. (1999), 'Right-wing socialist: an unlikely merger', *Central Europe Review* 1, 7 June.

Hugh, E. (2009), 'Devaluation, Euro membership, and loan defaults: some thoughts for my critics', *Baltic Economy Watch*. http://balticeconomy.blogspot.com/2009/03/devaluation-euro-membership-and-loan.html, accessed on 10 July 2010.

Huntington, S. (1993), 'The clash of civilizations?', *Foreign Affairs* 72, 3, pp. 22–49.

Huntington, S. (1996), 'The west unique, not universal', *Foreign Affairs* 75, 6, pp. 28–46.

Ilves, T.H. (1998), 'Estonia's Return to Europe', Estonian Ministry of Foreign Affairs, accessed at http://www.vm.ee/?q=en/node/3520.

Ilves, T. H. (1999), 'Estonia as a Nordic Country', Estonian Ministry of European Affairs, accessed at http://www.vm.ee/?q=node/3489.

International Monetary Fund (2013) 'Slovenia 2013 staff visit: concluding statement of the mission', http://www.imf.org/external/np/ms/2013/031813.htm, accessed on 9 December 2013.

International Monetary Fund (2013), 'Slovenia 2013 Staff Visit: Concluding Statement of the Mission', http: www.imf.org/external/np/ms/2013/031813d.htm, date accessed 9 May 2013.

Ivaldi, G. (2006), 'Beyond France's 2005 referendum on the European constitutional treaty: second-order model, anti-establishment attitudes and the end of the alternative European utopia', *West European Politics* 29, pp. 47–69.

Jabko, N. (2006), *Playing the Market: A Political Strategy for Uniting Europe, 1985-2005* (Ithaca: Cornell University Press).

Jackson, G. and Deeg, R. (2008), 'From comparing capitalisms to the politics of institutional change', *Review of International Political Economy* 15, pp. 680–709.

Jacoby, W. (2004), *The Enlargement of the European Union and NATO: Ordering from the Menu in Central Europe* (Cambridge: Cambridge University Press).

Jacoby, W. (2006), 'Inspiration, coalition and substitution: external influences on postcommunist transformations', *World Politics* 58, pp. 623–651.

Jacoby, W. (2014), 'The EU factor in fat times and in lean: did the EU amplify the boom and soften the bust?', *Journal of Common Market Studies* 52, pp. 52–70.

Jansen, S. C. (2008), 'Designer nations: neo-liberal nation branding – brand Estonia', *Social Identities* 14, pp. 121–142.

Kallaste, E. and Woolfson C. (2013), 'Negotiated responses to the crisis in the Baltic countries', *Transfer* 19, pp. 253–266.

Kangsepp, L. (2013), 'Ilves-Krugman spat to be turned into a "financial opera"', *Wall Street Journal*, 10 January.

Kaplinski, B. (2001), 'How accession to the European Union has affected external trade and foreign direct investment in Central European economies', *World Bank Policy Research Working Paper*, http://dx.doi.org/10.1596/1813-9450-2578.

Kattel, R. and Raudla R. (2013), 'The Baltic Republics and the crisis of 2008–2011', *Europe-Asia Studies* 65, pp. 426–449.

Keating, J. (2012), 'President of Estonia goes ballistic on Paul Krugman', *Foreign Policy* Passport blog, 6 June.

Kelley, J. (2004), *Ethnic Politics in Europe: The Power of Norms and Incentives* (Princeton: Princeton University Press).

Kiš, D. (1987), 'Variation on the theme of Central Europe', *Cross Currents: A Yearbook of Central European Culture* 6, pp. 1–14.

Kopecky, P. and Mudde C. (2002), 'The two sides of Euroscepticism: party positions on European integration in East Central Europe', *European Union Politics* 3, pp. 297–326.

KOKS et al. (2013), 'Slovenians demand radical change', http://criticallegalthinking.com/2013/01/15/slovenians-demand-radical-change/, date accessed 18 January 2013.

Krastev, I. (2013), 'What happened to the European dream?' *Vox Europ*, http://www.voxeurop.eu/en/content/article/3722191-what-happened-european-dream.

Krugman, P. (2012a), 'Estonian rhapsody', 'The conscience of a liberal', *The New York Times* blog, 6 June.

Krugman, P. (2012b), 'Ballistic in the Baltics', 'The conscience of a liberal' *The New York Times* blog, 7 June.

Kundera, M. (1984), 'The tragedy of Central Europe', *New York Review of Books*, 26 April.

Kurm, K. (2005), 'Defense minister suddenly resigns', *The Baltic Times*, 28 September, http://www.baltictimes.com/news/articles/13664/, date accessed 8 July 2006.

Kuus, M. (2002), 'European integration in identity narratives in Estonia: a quest for security', *Journal of Peace Research* 39, pp. 5–21.

Kuus, M. (2004), 'Europe's eastern expansion and the reinscription of otherness in East-Central Europe', *Progress in Human Geography* 28, pp. 472–489.

Kvist, J. (2004), 'Does EU enlargement start a race to the bottom? Strategic interaction among EU member states in social policy', *Journal of European Social Policy* 14, pp. 301–318.

Laar, M. (2002), *The Little Country that Could*. (London: Center for Research into Post-Communist Economics).

Lagerspetz, M. (1999), 'Postsocialism as a return: notes on a discursive strategy', *East European Politics and Societies* 13, pp. 377–390.
Lagerspetz, M. and Vogt, H. (1998), 'Estonia', in Aarebrot, F. (ed) *The Handbook of Political Change in Eastern Europe* (Cheltenham: Edward Elgar).
Lauristin, M. (1997), 'Contexts of Transition', in M. Lauristin and P. Vihalemm (eds) *Return to the Western World: Cultural and Political Perspectives on the Estonian Post-Communist Transition* (Tartu: Tartu University Press).
Lieberman, R. (2002), 'Ideas, institutions and political order: explaining political change' *American Political Science Review* 96, pp. 697–712.
Lieven, A. (1993), *Baltic Revolution: Estonia, Latvia, and Lithuania and the Path to Independence* (New Haven: Yale University Press).
Lindstrom, N. (2003), 'Between Europe and the Balkans: mapping Slovenia and Croatia's "return to Europe" in the 1990s', *Dialectical Anthropology* 27, pp. 313–329.
Lindstrom, N. (2006), 'Yugonostalgia: restorative and reflective nostalgia in former Yugoslavia' *East Central Europe/L'Europe du Center Est/Eine wissenschaftliche Zeitschrift* 32, 1–2, pp. 231–242.
Lindstrom, N. and Razsa M. (1998), 'Desnicu mije ili prepravijanje svetskog proetka' [The right hand washes the other: Huntington, Tudjman, and the new world order], *Arkzin* (Zagreb) 4, pp. 40–43.
Lindstrom, N. (2010), 'Service liberalization in the enlarged European Union: a race to the bottom or the emergence of transnational conflict?', *Journal of Common Market Studies* 10, pp. 1307–1327.
Lindstrom, N. (2011), 'Constitutionalism between Normative Frameworks and the Socio-Legal Frameworks of Societies', in Schiek D., Liebert U. and Schneider H. (eds) *European Economic and Social Constitutionalism after the Treaty of Lisbon* (Oxford: Oxford University Press).
Lindstrom, N. (2014), 'New Europe, enduring conflicts: the politics of European integration in the enlarged EU' (pp. 219–230) in Gould, A. and Messina, A. (eds) *Europe's Contending Identities: Supranationalism, Ethnoregionalism, Religion and New Nationalism* (Cambridge: Cambridge University Press).
Lindstrom, N. and Piroska D. (2007), 'The politics of privatization and Europeanization in Europe's periphery: Slovenian banks and breweries on sale', *Competition and Change* 11, pp. 117–135.

Lukšić, I. (1997), 'Interest Organizations in the Field of Social Partnership', in D. Fink-Hafner and J. Robbins (eds) *Making a New Nation: The Formation of Slovenia* (Farnham: Ashgate).

Lütz, S. and M. Kranke (2013), 'The European rescue of the Washington consensus? EU and IMF lending to Central and Eastern European countries', *Review of International Political Economy* 21, pp. 310–338.

Mair, P. (2004), 'The Europeanization dimension', *Journal of European Public Policy* 11, pp. 344–355.

Mair, P. (2007), 'Political opposition and the European Union', *Government and Opposition* 42, pp. 1–17.

Mair, P. and Zielonka J. (2002), *The Enlarged European Union: Diversity and Adaptation* (London: Frank Cass).

Marks, G. and Steenbergen M. (2004), *European Integration and Political Conflict* (Oxford: Oxford University Press).

Marks, G., Hooghe L., Nelson M., and Edwards E. (2006), 'Party competition and European integration in the East and West: different structure, same causality', *Comparative Political Studies* 39, pp. 155–175.

Mastenbroek, E. and Kaeding M. (2006), 'Europeanization beyond the goodness of fit: domestic politics in the forefront', *Comparative European Politics* 4, pp. 331–354.

Mekina, I. (2000), *Slovenia and the EU* (Ljubljana: Aim Press).

Mencinger, J. (2003), Does foreign direct investment always enhance economic growth, unpublished mimeo.

Menz, G. (2003), 'Re-regulating the single market: national varieties of capitalism and their responses to Europeanization', *Journal of European Public Policy* 10, pp. 532–555.

Mikkel, E. and Pridham G. (2004), 'Clinching the "return to Europe": the referendums on EU accession in Estonia and Latvia', *West European Politics* 27, pp. 716–748.

Myant, M. and Drahokoupil J. (2012), 'International integration, varieties of capitalism and resilience to crisis in transition economies', *Europe-Asia Studies* 64, pp. 1–33.

Neumann, I. (1999), *The Uses of the Other: The "East" in European Identity Formation* (Minneapolis: University of Minnesota Press).

Nölke, A. and Vliegenthart A. (2009), 'Enlarging the varieties of capitalism: the emergence of dependent market economies in East Central Europe', *World Politics* 61, pp. 670–702.

Norton, G. (2014), 'Slovenia freezes privatization as political campaigning heats up', *Business News Europe*, http://www.bne.eu/

content/slovenia-freezes-privatisation-political-campaigning-hots, date accessed 15 July 2014.
Novak, M. (2014a), 'Davos interview: Slovenian PM poll-leader wants to reconsider some privatizations', *Reuters*, 2 July 2014.
Novak, M. (2014b), 'Son of local hero bids to lead Slovenia to limited makeover', *Reuters*, 10 July 2014.
Novak, M. and Irish, J. (2014), 'Slovenian PM Bratusek resigns, wants early election' *Reuters*, 5 May.
O'Dwyer, C. and Kovalčík B. (2007), 'And the last shall be first: party system institutionalization and second-generation economic reform in postcommunist Europe', *Studies in Comparative International Development* 41, pp. 3–26.
Offe, C. (1991), 'Capitalism by democratic design? Democratic theory facing the triple transition in East Central Europe', *Social Research* 58, pp. 865–892.
Orenstein, M. (2001), *Out of the Red: Building Capitalism and Democracy in Postcommunist Europe* (Ann Arbor: University of Michigan Press).
Organisation for Economic Co-operation and Development (2013), *OECD Economic Surveys: Slovenia* (Paris: OECD).
Parsons, C. (2003), *A Certain Idea of Europe* (Ithaca: Cornell University Press).
Patterson, P. (2003), 'On the edge of reason: the boundaries of Balkanism in Slovenian, Austrian and Italian discourse', *Slavic Review* 62, pp. 110–141.
Petrin, T. (1995), *Industrial Policy Supporting Economic Transition in Central-Eastern Europe: Lessons from Slovenia* (Berkeley: University of California Press).
Pickel, A. (2005), 'Introduction: false oppositions', in Helleiner E. and Pickel A. (eds) *Economic Nationalism in a Globalizing World* (Ithaca: Cornell University Press).
Pierson, P. (1998), 'Irresistible forces, immovable objects: post-industrial welfare states confront permanent austerity', *Journal of European Public Policy* 5, pp. 539–560.
Piroska, D. (2002), 'Varieties of debt management in Central and East European countries', *Copenhagen Business School Working Paper*, pp. 2004–2074.
Polanyi, K. (2001) [1944], *The Great Transformation: The Political and Economic Origins of our Time* (Boston: Beacon Press).

Proos, P. (2010), 'Estonia's euro opponent: Estonia is getting the last ticket for the Titanic', Press release, 30 December. www.teameurope.info/node/791, date accessed 17 July 2013.

Quaglia, L. (2010), 'Completing the single market in financial services: the politics of competing advocacy coalitions', *Journal of European Public Policy* 17, pp. 1007–1023.

Radaelli, C. (2003), 'The Europeanization of Public Policy', in K. Featherstone and C. Radaelli (eds) *The Politics of Europeanization* (Oxford: Oxford University Press).

Raig, I. (2002), 'Impact of EU accession to Estonia's development', *Institute for European Studies Proceedings* 1.1. (Tallinn: Institute for European Studies).

Raig, I. (2003), 'Time for closer transatlantic cooperation' *EU Observer*, 5 February.

Raik, K. (2004), 'EU accession of Central and Eastern European countries: democracy and integration as conflicting logics', *East European Politics and Societies* 18, pp. 567–594.

Raudla, R. and Kattel R. (2011), 'Why did Estonia choose fiscal retrenchment after the 2008 crisis?', *Journal of Public Policy* 31, pp. 163–186.

Ray, L. (2004), 'Don't Rock the Boat: Expectations, Fears, and Opposition to EU-level Policy Making', in G. Marks and M. R. Steenbergen (eds) *European Integration and Political Conflict* (Cambridge: Cambridge University Press).

Razsa, M. and N. Lindstrom (2004), 'Balkan is beautiful: Balkanism in the political discourse of Tudjman's Croatia', *East European Politics and Societies* 18, pp. 628–650.

Razsa, M. and Kurnik A. (2012), 'The occupy movement in Žižek's hometown: direct democracy and a politics of becoming', *American Ethnologist* 39, pp. 238–258.

Reuters (2008), 'IMF, OECD urge privatization of Slovenian banks', 11 November.

Risse, T. (2001), 'A European Identity? Europeanization and the Evolution of Nation-State Identities', in Cowles M. G., Caporaso J. and Risse T. (eds) *Transforming Europe: Europeanization and Domestic Change* (Ithaca: Cornell University Press).

Rousek, L. (2013), 'Slovenian lawmakers approve privatization plan', *The Wall Street Journal*, 21 June.

Ruggie, J. G. (1982), 'International regimes, transactions, and change: embedded liberalism in the post-war economic order', *International Organization* 36, pp. 379–415.

Rupel, D. (2000), 'Slovenian foreign policy, 1991–2001', unpublished manuscript.

Sasse, G. (2008), 'The politics of EU conditionality: the norm of minority protection during and beyond EU accession', *Journal of European Public Policy* 15, pp. 842–860.

Scharpf, F. (2002), 'The European Social Model: Coping with the Challenges of Diversity', *Journal of Common Market Studies*, 40, 645–670.

Schimmelfennig, F. (2001) 'The community trap: liberal norms, rhetorical action, and the eastern enlargement of the European Union', *International Organization* 55, pp. 47–80.

Schimmelfennig, F., Engert S., and Knobel H. (2003), 'Costs, commitment and compliance: the impact of EU democratic conditionality on Latvia, Slovakia, and Turkey', *Journal of Common Market Studies* 41, pp. 495–518.

Schimmelfennig, F. and Sedelmeier U. (2004), 'Governance by conditionality: EU rule transfer to the candidate countries of Central and Eastern Europe', *Journal of European Public Policy* 11, pp. 661–679.

Schimmelfennig, F. and Sedelmeier U. (eds) (2005), *The Europeanization of Central and Eastern Europe* (Ithaca: Cornell University Press).

Schmidt, V. (2006), *Democracy in Europe* (Oxford: Oxford University Press).

Schmidt, V. (2010), 'Taking ideas and discourse seriously: explaining change through discursive institutionalism as the fourth "new institutionalism"', *European Political Science Review* 2, pp. 1–25.

Schöpflin, G. and Wood N. (1989), *In Search of Central Europe* London: Polity.

Sedelmeier, U. (2009), "Europeanisation in new member and candidate states." *Living Review of European Governance*. Accessed at: http://www.livingreviews.org/lreg-2006-3.

Sedelmeier, U. (2012) 'Is Europeanisation through conditionality sustainable? Lock-in of institutional change after EU Accession', *West European Politics* 35, pp. 20–38.

Sissenich, B. (2007), *Building States without Societies: European Union Enlargement and the Transfer of EU Social Policy to Poland and Hungary* (New York: Lexington Books).

Skov, H. (2005) 'No! to EU: debate in Estonia', http://manila.djh.dk/Euestonia/stories, date accessed 1 January 2006.

Slovenia Business Week (2001), 'Bank privatization stirs up heated debate', 12 November.

Slovenia Business Week (2002a), 'Balance between Slovenian and foreign capital is important', 14 January.

Slovenian Business Week (2002b), 'European ommission trusts Slovenian anti-trust authorities', 14 December.

Slovenian Council (2013), 'An Ooen letter by the Slovenian Council for the Republic to institutions in Europe and the world', email, date accessed 22 January 2013.

Slovenian National Assembly (1999), Declaration of Slovenian foreign policy, unpublished document, accessed 15 September 2002.

Slovenian Press Agency (2009), 'Infond holding files lawsuit against creditor banks', 3 November.

Slovenian Press Agency (2010), 'Daily says economic crisis saved Slovenia from Sot', 13 March.

Smith, B. (2001), 'Estonia's Euroskepticism', *Estonian Advantage*, p. 9.

Smith, D. (2002), 'Estonia: Independence and European Integration', in D. Smith (ed.) *The Baltic States: Estonia, Latvia, and Lithuania* (London: Routledge).

Sommers, J. and Woolfson, C. (2014) *The Contradictions of Austerity: The Socio-Economic Costs of the Neoliberal Baltic Model* (London: Routledge).

Sovdat, P. and Urbas U. (2010), 'Intervju – Borut Pahor: Lani je Slovenijo tresla križa, zdaj jo bodo reforme [Last year Slovenia shaking from crisis, now they will reform], *Finance*, 17 May.

Stanovnik, S. (2011), 'Guest post: Slovenia's leaders must respond to global turmoil with privatization', Beyondbrics, *Financial Times*, date accessed 22 August 2011.

Stanojević, M. and Klarič M. (2013), 'The impact of socio-economic shocks on social dialogue in slovenia', *Transfer* 19, pp. 217–226.

Statistical Office of the Republic of Slovenia (2010), *Statistical Yearbook of the Republic of Slovenia* (Ljubljana: Statistical Office of the Republic of Slovenia).

Statistics Estonia (2010), 'Poverty in Estonia', www.stat.ee/38022, date accessed 12 July 2012.

Stavovnik, S. (2012), 'Guest post: Slovenia's playtime is over', Beyondbrics, *Financial Times*, 6 September 2012.

Stojaspal, J. (2004), 'Want lower taxes: go east' *Time*, 11 July.

Štor, B. (2010), 'Exit strategy: light at the end of the tunnel?', *Slovenian Times*, 5 March.

Streeck, W. (2011), 'The crises of democratic capitalism', *New Left Review* 71, pp. 5–29.
Svetličič, M. and Rojec M. (2003), *Facilitating Transition by Internationalization: Outward Direct Investment from Central European Economies* (London: Ashgate).
Szacki, J. (1995), *Liberalism after Communism* (Budapest: Central European University Press).
Szczerbiak, A. and Taggart P. (2008), *Opposing Europe? The Comparative Party Politics of Euroscepticism. Volume 2: Comparative and Theoretical Perspectives* (Oxford: Oxford University Press).
Taagepera, R. (1993), *Estonia: Return to Independence* (Boulder, CO: Westview Press).
Tarn, M. (2003), 'Euro-Doubts' *City Paper: The Baltic States* ,15 June.
Tere, J. (2009), 'Edgar Savisaar: none of Ansip's forecasts or promises come true', *The Baltic Course*, 22 May.
Tere, J. (2010), 'EU's least indebted state Estonia is model for Euro after Greek crisis', *The Baltic Course*, 11 May.
The Baltic Course (2009), 'Trade unions to organize protest against Estonian government', 26 May.
The XX Committee, 'Slovenia's bailout, with a side of Schadenfreude' 20committee.com/2012/09/15/slovenias-bailout-with-a-side-of-schadenfreude, date accessed 13 May 2013.
Thorhallsson, B. and Kattel R. (2013), 'Neo-liberal small states and economic crisis: lessons for democratic corporatism', *Journal of Baltic Studies* 44, pp. 83–103.
Tilly, C. (1998), 'Epilogue: Now Where?' in Steinmetz, G. (ed.) *State/Culture: State-Formation after the Cultural Turn* (Ithaca, NY: Cornell University Press).
Todorova, M. (1997), *Imagining the Balkans* (Oxford: Oxford University Press).
TV Slovenija 1 (2005), Live news broadcast, 17 January.
Vachudova, M. (2005), *Europe Undivided: Democracy, Leverage, and Integration after Communism* (Oxford: Oxford University Press).
Vasilopoulou, S. (2013), 'Continuity and change in the study of Euroscepticism: plus şa change?' *Journal of Common Market Studies* 51, pp. 153–168.
Vaughan-Whitehead, D. (2003), *EU Enlargement versus Social Europe? The Uncertain Future of the European Social Model* (London: Edward Elgar).
Vezovnik, A. (2010), 'Krekism and the Construction of Slovenian National Identity: Newspaper Commentaries on Slovenia's European

Union Integration', in Šarić L., Musolff A., Manz S. (eds) *Contesting Europe's Eastern Rim: Cultural Identities in Public Discourse* (Bristol: Multilingual Matters).

Viktorova, J. (2007), 'Conflict transformation the Estonian way: the Estonian-Russian border conflict, European integration and shifts in discursive representation of "the other"', *Perspectives* 27, pp. 44–66.

Wæver, O. (1992), 'Nordic nostalgia: northern Europe after the Cold War', *International Affairs* 68, pp. 77–102.

Wedel, J. (2001), *Collision and Collusion: The Strange Case of Western Aid to Eastern Europe* (New York: Palgrave Macmillan).

Wilde, P. and Trenz H. J. (2012), 'Denouncing European integration: Euroscepticism as polity contestation', *European Journal of Social Theory* 15, pp. 537–554.

Wincott, D. (2003), 'The Idea of the European Social Model: Limits and Paradoxes of Europeanization', in Featherstone K. and Radaelli C. (eds) *The Politics of Europeanization* (Oxford: Oxford University Press).

Wolff, L. (1994), *Inventing Eastern Europe: The Map of Civilization in the Mind of the Enlightenment* (Stanford: Stanford University Press).

World Economic Forum (2004), 'The Lisbon Review: An Assessment of Policies and Reforms in Europe'. http: www.weforum.org/pdf/Gcr/LisbonReview/Lisbon_Review_2004.pdf, date accessed 10 July 2005.

Žižek, S. (2013), 'The West's crisis is one of democracy as much as finance', *The Guardian*, 16 January.

Index

acqui communitaire, 38, 40, 47
active leverage, 34, 36
actor density, 37
adoption costs, 36–7, 38, 44
agricultural policy, 39
Alpe-Adria, 21, 29
Ansip, Andrus, 61, 62
applicant states, 35
    EU influence on, 35–7
    resistance by, to EU rules, 39–40
    rule compliance by, 35, 38–9
architects of transition, 3, 33, 42, 51, 75
austerity, 57–60, 62, 65–8, 71–2
Austria, 29

Baltic cooperation, 24–5
Baltic Council, 25
Baltic States, 20, 27–9, 40–1, 58
Baltic Way, 25
banking regulation, 34, 63
bank privatization, 47–9, 65–6, 69–71
Berlin Wall, fall of, 18
Bohle, Dorothee, 2, 3, 12, 13, 14, 42, 45, 50, 51, 55, 58
borderland discourses, 20
Bosnia, 45
Bratušek, Alenka, 68–70, 71
Bruszt, László, 39
budget deficits, 56, 66–7
Bulgaria, 75
Bush, George W., 55, 63

capital investments, 55
capitalist models, 2–4, 6, 12, 46, 52, 54, 57, 71–2, 76
Carantania, 27–9
Center Party (Estonia), 59–60
Central and Eastern Europe (CEE)
    as on border of Europe, 19–21
    as center of Europe, 18–19, 23, 27
    economic boom period for, 54–6
    EU accession process and, 34–52
    as European, 17–32
    EU rule adoption in, 11
    impact of financial crisis on, 53–73
    nation-state building in, 13, 50–1
    politics of Europeanization in, 10–13
    post-socialist transformations in, 2–4, 11–13, 75–7
    'return to Europe' by, 18–22
    as sub-region of Europe, 21–2, 24–6, 29–31
central bank dependence, 39
Central European Free Trade Area (CEFTA), 21
Central European Initiative, 21
centrally planned economies, 40–1

Cerar, Miro, 70–1
Christianity, 32
civil society, 10, 13, 35
Clash of Civilizations, 20–1, 23–4
class conflicts, 73
Clinton, Bill, 27–8
Cold War, 18, 21
Communist Party (Estonia), 41
communist regimes, demise of, 2
comparative political economy, 75–6
compliance, with EU rules, 11, 35–40
conditionality, 2, 3, 33–52
Copenhagen Criteria, 38
Czech Republic, 12, 19

Damijan, Joze, 63
Dayton Agreement, 30
Debeljak, Aleš, 30
democratic capitalism, 54, 77
democratic reforms, 34, 35
Denmark, 9
dependent market economies, 12
deregulation, 2, 11, 55
differentiation process, 20–1, 23–4
discursive strategies, 76–7
dissent, 16, 66–8, 72
domestic actors, 10, 13, 36, 58–9
domestic adoption costs, 36–7, 38, 44
domestic change, 2, 35, 37–9

Eastern Europe, see Central and Eastern Europe (CEE)
economic growth, 54–6
economic integration, 8
economic nationalism, 13–16, 51, 75
economy
    of Estonia, 40–1, 54, 57–62
    of Slovenia, 45–50, 63–7
    state intervention in, 6, 11, 41, 46, 54, 64, 71
elites, 6, 10, 13–16, 18, 43, 46, 50–1, 74–7
embedded neoliberal model, 12
environmental policy, 34
Epstein, R., 39
Estonia, 3, 77
    architects of transition in, 42–3
    austerity measures in, 58–60, 62, 71–2
    banking sector in, 58
    contestation by, 40–5
    discursive strategies of, to return to Europe, 22–6, 40
    economy of, 40–1, 54, 57–62
    EU accession process and, 43–5, 61
    impact of financial crisis on, 3–4, 57–62, 71–3
    market model in, 12
    neoliberal policies in, 41–5, 57–62
    Russian-speaking minority in, 23–4, 41–2
    Soviet Union and, 40, 41–2, 51
    transition strategy of, 3, 40–5
Estonian identity, 23, 32, 52, 61
Estonian Trade Union Confederation (EAKL), 59
euro, 56, 61–2, 73
Europe
    borders of, 18, 19–21, 31
    center of, 18–19, 23, 27
    definition of, 18
    politics of, 17–32
    'return' to, 18–22, 31–2, 40, 51
    sub-regions of, 21–2, 24–6, 29–31
European Commission, 21, 35, 38–9, 47, 48, 56, 68
European identity, 19, 20, 29, 32
European integration, 5–9
    debate on, in CEE, 10–13
    goals of, 9
    ideational context of, 76
    opposition to, 9
Europeanization, 2, 4, 6, 76
    in CEE, 10–13
    by EU conditionality, 34–8
    politics of, 5–16
    top-down, 38–9
European Parliament, 6–7
European social model, 8, 11, 55, 57, 73, 77
European Union (EU), 2
    accession process, 10–11, 21–2, 34–52, 61

European Union (EU) – *continued*
  conditionality, 2, 3, 33–52
  contestation of, 5–10, 40–50
  economic boom period for, 54–6
  enlargment of, 54–7
  impact of financial crisis on, 56–7
  opposition to, 43–5, 61–2
  rule compliance in, 35
Euroskepticism, 9
external incentives model, 35–7

financial sector regulations, 56
Finland, 9, 25
fiscal crisis, 56–8
fiscal policy, 54, 61
flat tax, 55
foreign banks, 47–9, 55, 58
foreign direct investment (FDI), 49–50
free markets, 8, 13, 34, 41, 42, 44, 50, 54

Gaspari, Mitja, 66
Germany, 9
global financial crisis, impact of, 3–4, 53–73
globalization, 12
'goodness of fit', 38
Gourevitch, P., 37
Gräzin, Igor, 44
Greskovits, Béla, 2, 3, 12, 13, 14, 42, 45, 50, 51, 55
Greece, 61

Hanseatic League, 23
Hapsburg Empire, 29
Havel, Vaclav, 21
Hendrik, Toomas, 62
Hooghe, L., 7–8, 9
Hungary, 12, 19, 56
Huntington, S., 20–1, 23, 32

Iceland, 58
Ilves, T. H., 25–6
Independence Party (UK), 8
institutionalist approach, 76
International Monetary Fund (IMF), 11, 45, 46–7, 56, 66, 69, 72

Italy, 29, 47
Jacoby, W., 37
Jankovic, Zoran, 67

Janša, Janez, 63, 67
Križanic, Franc, 65–6
Krugman, Paul, 62
Kučan, Milan, 27
Kundera, M., 19
Kuus, M., 32

Laar, Mart, 42
labor policy, 36–7
labor unions, 10, 13, 59, 66, 71–2
Laško brewey, 49, 64
Latvia, 25, 36, 56, 57
Lauristin, Marju, 23
League of Nations, 22
legitimacy, 39–40, 42, 64, 71, 73
Lehman Brothers, 56, 64
liberal democracy, 36
Liberal Democratic Party (LDS) (Slovenia), 45–6
Lisbon Agenda, 63
Lithuania, 25, 26
Logi, Jurgen, 58

market economy, 3
market integration, 8
market liberalization, 10, 11, 13, 41, 42
market-making principles, 6, 9, 73
market-shaping principles, 6, 9
Marks, G., 7–8, 9
Mekina, I., 31
membership conditionality, 2, 3, 33–52
member states, 35
Mencinger, Joze, 46–9
Meri, Lennart, 23, 24
minority rights, 34, 35
monetary policy, 54

national chauvinism, 19
National Council (Slovenia), 46
national identity, 23, 32, 50–2, 61, 75
nationalism, 15
  see also economic nationalism
national market liberal model, 8, 75

national social model, 8, 75
nation-state building, 13, 50–1
negative integration, 40
neo-corporatist model, 12
neo-liberalism, 2, 7–9, 11, 12, 41–5, 51, 55, 57, 63, 77
nesting orientalisms, 20
Noric region, 25
normative consistency, 39
'No to the EU Movement', 43
Nova Kreditna Banka Maribor (NKBM), 47–8
Nova Ljubljanska Banka (NLB), 47, 65–6

Occupy movement, 56
Orenstein, Mitchell, 12, 42, 55, 77

Parts, Juhan, 58
passive leverage, 34, 36
Peterle, Alojz, 46
Pivovarna Union brewery, 49
Poland, 12, 19
political conflict, 2–3
political contention, 6–10
political economy, 10, 15, 75–6
political parties, 7, 10, 13, 41, 45–6, 59–60
politics
 of conditionality, 33–52
 of crisis, 53–73
 of "Europe", 17–32
 of Europeanization, 5–16
Poolamets, Anti, 61
post-socialist transformations, 2–4, 11–13, 34, 75–7
privatization, 2, 11, 41, 45, 47–50, 65, 69, 71
Proos, Peeter, 61
Pro Patria party (Estonia), 41, 42
public opinion, 7, 9, 10, 61–2

Raig, Ivan, 43–4
Reform Party (Estonia), 59, 62
regional associations, 21–2, 24–6, 29–31
regulated capitalism, 7–8, 9

Research Center Free Europe, 44
'return to Europe', 18–22, 31–2, 40, 51
Romania, 56, 75
Ross, Märten, 58
Rupel, Dmitri, 28
Russian 'other', 19, 24, 41–2

Sarkozy, Nicolas, 55
Savisaar, Edgar, 59–60
Schimmelfennig, Frank, 34, 35, 36
second generation reforms, 55–6, 63
Sedelmeier, Ulrich, 34, 35, 37, 40
Semolic, Dušan, 66
Serbia, 45
shock therapy, 11, 13, 41, 42
Silberg, Uno, 43
Single European Act, 6
Slovakia, 12, 36
Slovenia, 3, 58, 77
 austerity measures in, 65–8, 71–2
 banking sector in, 47–9, 63–6, 69–70
 brewing industry in, 49–50
 discursive strategies of, to return to Europe, 27–31
 economic policies, 45–51, 63–7
 elites in, 46, 48–9
 EU accession process and, 47–50
 fiscal crisis in, 3–4
 foreign direct investment in, 49–50
 foreign policy of, 28–9
 growth in, 54
 impact of financial crisis on, 62–73
 market model in, 12
 neoliberal policies in, 51, 63
 protests in, 66–8, 72
 transition strategy of, 3, 45–50, 75–6
Slovenian Central Bank, 47
Slovenian Democratic Party (SDS), 66, 70–1
Slovenian identity, 52
Social Democratic Party (Estonia), 59, 60
social dumping, 55
socialism, 2, 35
social policy, 36–7, 54
social protections, 8, 9

sovereignty, 7, 44, 61
Soviet Union, 19, 22, 24, 40–3, 51
state intervention, in economy, 6, 11, 41, 46, 54, 64, 71
Streeck, W., 73
supranational institutions, 7, 10, 11
Sweden, 2, 9, 52
Swedish banks, 58

Taliga, Harri, 59
Tarand, Indrek, 59
tariffs, 41, 42
technocratic intellectual elites, 6, 13, 15–16, 43, 46, 48–50
Tilly, C., 15
Todorova, M., 29
trade barriers, 42, 45
trade liberalization, 41, 42
trade unions, 10, 13, 59, 66, 71–2
transnational capitalisms, 12–13

unemployment, 55, 57
United Kingdom, 2, 9, 26, 52, 58

Vachudova, Milada, 3, 34, 35, 36
varieties of capitalism, 9–10, 12, 14–15, 52, 76
Visegrád Group, 21
voucher capitalists, 46, 47

wages, 55, 66
Warsaw Pact, 19
welfare capitalism, 2, 4, 6, 9–10, 12, 13, 15, 16, 44, 46, 50, 52, 54, 64, 74–6
Western civilization, 20–1, 24, 32
Western Europe, 2, 11, 18, 34, 45, 75
World War II, 28

Yugoslavia, 30, 32, 45
Yule-land, 25–6

Lightning Source UK Ltd.
Milton Keynes UK
UKOW04n2322191214

243425UK00003B/9/P